Produced by AA Publishing

Captions by Richard Cavendish

Filmset by Wyvern Typesetting Ltd, Bristol
Origination by Scantrans Pte Ltd, Singapore
Printed and bound by New Interlitho SpA, Italy

The contents of this publication are believed correct
at the time of printing. Nevertheless, the publishers
cannot accept responsibility for errors or omissions,
or for changes in details given.

A CIP catalogue record for this book is available
from the British Library.

Published by The Automobile Association, Fanum
House, Basing View, Basingstoke, Hampshire
RG21 2EA.

ISBN 0 7495 0149 9

Front cover: Top – *Forth Bridges, looking north*
Main – *Loch Alsh and Eilean Donan Castle*
Back cover: *Dochart Falls, Killin, and Ben Lawers
in the distance*
Title page (opposite): *Ben Lawers and Loch Tay,
Tayside*

AA

visions·of
SCOTLAND

Visions of Scotland is a celebration in words and pictures of a beautiful country. This collection of photographs is designed to create an atmosphere which encapsulates Scotland in all its moods and seasons.

Scotland

Opposite right *The wearing of Highland costume was forbidden by law after the 1745 uprising, but the ban was withdrawn in 1782 and kilts and tartans became a central element of the 19th-century image of 'romantic Scotland'.*

Below *Tartans, or chequered patterns, have a long history in Scotland, going back before the Middle Ages. Today each Highland clan has its own distinctive 'sett' or tartan pattern.*

Right *A piper in his finery of kilt and bonnet. The old Highland all-purpose garment cum blanket was the plaid, which was wrapped round the body and belted at the waist. The pleated kilt came in during the 18th century when the plaid, in effect, was divided in two.*

Previous spread *Wild cat, eagle and red deer haunt lofty Beinn Eighe in the wilds of Wester Ross in the Highlands, above Glen Torridon. This is the site of Britain's first National Nature Reserve, established in 1951.*

Left *Scene at Nether Mill in the Borders. There are now over 200 officially recognized tartan patterns distinctive to clans, Scottish regiments, districts or clan chiefs and their immediate kinsmen.*

Left *Visitors admiring 'the Queen's View' over rippling Loch Tummel with the 3547ft (1081m) hump of Schiehallion, 'the fairy hill', rising in the background. Queen Victoria visited here in 1866, but the viewpoint is probably named after Mary, Queen of Scots, who admired this prospect over 300 years before.*

Below *A tartan hat and the red lion state a claim to Scottish identity. The red lion rampant was the heraldic badge of the kings of Scots.*

Left *A waterfall in the Pass of Glencoe. Scotland's most famous glen is known for its mountain scenery, with peaks above 3000ft (914m), and for the treacherous massacre of Macdonalds by Campbells on a freezing February night in 1692. Much of the glen is now cared for by the National Trust for Scotland.*

Following spread *Looking over the gleaming River Tay at Kinnoull Hill, near Perth. The tower is a folly, built by an Earl of Kinnoull in the 18th century in imitation of the Rhine castles. The hill commands spectacular views of the Tay.*

11

Scotland

Above *Casks of the noble fluid maturing in the Glenfiddich Whisky Distillery at Dufftown, Grampian. The distillery, which dates from the 1880s, is open to visitors most of the year.*

Right *Stills create an eerily Martian scene in the Glenfiddich Distillery. The taste of malt whisky differs between distilleries as little as half a mile apart, due to minute variations in soil and water conditions.*

Left *Toy yachts, windmills and Scots gnomes outside a house at Stonehaven, formerly a major fishing port on the east coast, south of Aberdeen. The once prosperous Scottish fishing industry has declined in recent years.*

Above *The quay at Pennan on the Buchan coast, where the whitewashed cottages shelter at the foot of formidable sandstone cliffs.*

Left *Fishing boats are reflected in the water at Mallaig, on the western coast of the Lochaber district, a port for Skye and the Inner Hebrides.*

Scotland

Right *Fishing dinghies in repose at Ballantrae, on the west coast. Despite the name, this is not the real setting of Robert Louis Stevenson's* Master of Ballantrae.

Bottom right *Fishing buoys dangle over the side of a boat at Fraserburgh, a former herring port on the Buchan stretch of the Grampian Region coast. The town is named after a local laird who lived here in the 16th century.*

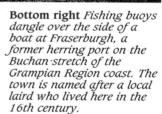

Above *The fishing port of Arbroath on the east coast. The town is famous for its 'smokies' (smoked haddock) and the Declaration of Arbroath in 1320 – perhaps the most notable statement of Scotland's independence. In the background is the Signal Tower, now a museum of local history and the fishing industry.*

Following spread *Looking across Loch Duich to the steep and comely peaks called the Five Sisters of Kintail, in an area of Wester Ross owned by the National Trust for Scotland. Sgurr Fhuaran rises to 3505ft, (1068m).*

22

Right *A simple whitewashed cottage makes an effective backdrop for its garden at Port Ramsay on the island of Lismore, 'the great garden', in Loch Linnhe.*

Left *A Border shepherd with his dogs. In the background lies the Talla Reservoir in the valley of the Tweed south-west of Peebles.*

Above *The narrow mountain pass of Bealach na Ba, near Applecross in Wester Ross, snakes its way up above 2000ft (610m) through a bleak landscape of stone and scree between Sgurr a'Chaorachain and Meall Gorm, 'the blue mountain'.*

Above *Scotland has a high reputation for fine textiles, and quality products can be seen and bought at the Scottish Craft Centre at Acheson House in Edinburgh.*

Right *A variety of products of the 19th-century Clock Mill at Tillicoultry, north-east of Stirling in the Central Region.*

Below *A potter at work in New Lanark. This late 18th-century spinning village on the River Clyde has been restored as a craft complex.*

Above *Textiles and other craft products in the Granite Square shop in the small Lochaber town of Strontian (which ominously gave its name to Strontium-90).*

Left *Kilbarchan, near Paisley in Strathclyde, was once famous for its tartans. Traditional home weaving is demonstrated on looms at the Weaver's Cottage, owned by the National Trust for Scotland.*

Following spread *Waterfall at the head of Alva Glen, a beauty spot at the foot of the romantic Ochil Hills, in the Central Region, with a path to the 2363ft (720m) summit of Ben Cleuch.*

28

Above *The grim and ancient Torridon peaks glower above Loch Torridon in the north-western Highlands. This is famous and dangerous mountaineering country.*

Above *Monarch of all he surveys: the snowy Cuillin peaks form a dramatic background to the scenery near Elgol in the Isle of Skye. Rising well above 3000ft (914m), the Cuillins (pronounced 'Coolins') provide exciting but treacherous climbing.*

Left *Traffic negotiates the 1930s road through the Pass of Glencoe beside the tumbling River Coe. This is a splendid area for walking and climbing.*

29

Following spread *Looking west along Loch Garry, with the wild hills of Knoydart in the distance. A minor road runs through entrancing Highland scenery along Loch Garry and Loch Quoich to Loch Hourn.*

Scotland

Right *Scotland's museums illuminate every aspect of the country's life: including its wildlife, as in this nostalgic stained glass window, 'The Hills of Home', in the Deer Museum in the Galloway Forest Park.*

Right *The Highland crofter's life is preserved at Laidhay Croft Museum near Dunbeath. Family and farm animals lived under the same roof here.*

Above *Figures from Edinburgh's past: the 16th-century Huntly House in Canongate, Edinburgh, is now a lively museum of the city's history.*

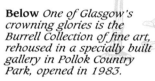

Left (top) *Historic cars, commercial vehicles and advertising signs keep the past vividly alive at the Myreton Motor Museum, near Aberlady, Lothian.*

Below *One of Glasgow's crowning glories is the Burrell Collection of fine art, rehoused in a specially built gallery in Pollok Country Park, opened in 1983.*

33

Far left *Silver-mounted sporran and dirk at the Inverness Museum and Art Gallery. The sporran is a purse made of an animal's skin, with the hair left on, and ornamental tassels.*

Left *The Weaver's Cottage at Kilbarchan preserves the way of life of the local cottage industry.*

Scotland

Left *The fishing in Scotland is among the best in Britain, with salmon and trout plentiful in rivers and lochs. This angler is fishing the River Spey at Craigellachie. The bridge is by Thomas Telford and was opened in 1815. The Speyside Walk follows the river.*

Above *Lochearnhead in the Central Region is a focus for water-skiing and watersports on Loch Earn, a beautiful loch 7 miles (11km) long and set among stately mountains. Glen Ogle leads north into the Highlands.*

Scotland

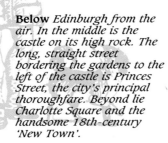

Right *Royal Edinburgh: the capital city of Scotland is home to the historic Stuart palace of Holyrood House. This lantern at the entrance is topped by a crown.*

Below *Edinburgh from the air. In the middle is the castle on its high rock. The long, straight street bordering the gardens to the left of the castle is Princes Street, the city's principal thoroughfare. Beyond lie Charlotte Square and the handsome 18th-century 'New Town'.*

Above *Lauriston Castle, beside the Forth, is a 16th-century tower house built by one of the Napier family (father of the inventor of logarithms, John Napier of Merchiston). The house was enlarged in the 19th century and contains a good collection of art objects and furniture.*

Right *The 1840s monument to Sir Walter Scott, on Princes Street. Beneath the Gothic canopy is a statue of Sir Walter with his dog Maida, surrounded by figures from his novels.*

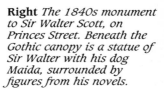

Above *Behind the ornamental fountain is Edinburgh Castle, perched up on its great basalt rock. Today it is more of a palace cum barracks than a fortress of the conventional kind, with the royal regalia of Scotland on display, the apartments of Mary, Queen of Scots and the Scottish National War Memorial.*

Left *'I'm not dead yet': memorial in Paisley Close to a brave young man who was trapped under a collapsing building in 1861 and encouraged his rescuers.*

Scotland

Previous spread *Snow lies deep and fleecy on Ben Lawers, viewed from across Loch Tay in the Breadalbane district of the Grampian Mountains. From the summit you can see right across Scotland, to the Atlantic in one direction and the North Sea in the other.*

Right *The rugged grandeur of Scotland's castles matches the beauty of the natural scenery. The ruined Campbell fastness of Kilchurn Castle in Argyll, its keep dating from the 15th century, is seen across Loch Awe, with Ben Cruachan majestic in the background.*

Below *Dunnottar Castle crouches on its seagirt rock, on the east coast, south of Stonehaven. Dominated by its 14th-century keep, this old stronghold of the Earls Marischal has a dark past and many prisoners perished in its dungeons.*

Left *Mellerstain House, a handsome Georgian mansion near Kelso, in the Borders, was designed by William and Robert Adam for the Baillie family. There are sumptuous interiors in the Adam manner.*

Above *Queen Victoria used to sleep in this bedroom on her visits to Scone Palace, near Perth. Scone (pronounced 'Skoon') was once the capital of the Picts. The present palace dates from the early 1800s.*

Left *Bells to summon the army of servants at Hopetoun House near South Queensferry in Lothian, the stately 18th-century residence of the Marquesses of Linlithgow.*

41

Scotland

Above *In a moonlike landscape of stony desolation in Wester Ross, a cairn of stones provides a commanding viewpoint beside the mountain pass of Bealach na Ba.*

Right *Looking north from Rough Knowe on one of the Border drove roads, used by cattlemen to take their herds to market, and also no doubt by cattle thieves. Rustling was endemic in the Borders and many a cow trod many a weary mile to and fro.*

Left *Cutting peat on Charlie's Moss near Langholm in Dumfries and Galloway. Peat is Scotland's traditional fuel, cut with a spade into blocks which are spread out to dry: in its natural state it may contain up to 95 per cent water.*

Below *This medieval stained glass window is now in the Burrell Collection in Glasgow. The collection was formed by a Glasgow shipping magnate, Sir William Burrell, who donated it to the city in 1944.*

Right *This cross in the church at Ruthwell, just across the border from Carlisle, is a major monument of early Christianity in Britain. Standing 18ft (5½m) high, it was carved in the 7th or 8th century with scenes from the life of Christ, Latin inscriptions, vine foliage, birds and animals. Verses from an Old English poem, 'The Dream of the Rood', are cut on the cross in Northumbrian runes.*

Below *A crudely vigorous gargoyle protrudes from the side of the imposing medieval church of St Mary at Haddington in Lothian, a market town noted for its 18th-century streets and houses, and as the birthplace of John Knox.*

Above *One of the mysterious Pictish carved stones at Aberlemno, near Brechin in Tayside. The intricate carvings are thought to date from the period AD600 to 900. The Picts, or 'painted people' of eastern and north-eastern Scotland, were probably descended from non-Celtic aboriginal inhabitants.*

Following spread *The entry to the ominous Pass of Glencoe, whose name means 'glen of weeping'. The valley is hemmed in by towering peaks built up of volcanic lava flows and rising above 3000ft (914m): Buchaille Etive Mor ('The Great Shepherd of Etive'), Buchaille Etive Beag ('The Little Shepherd'), the Three Sisters of Glencoe and Bidean nam Bian ('The Peak of the Bens'), which stands 3766ft (1147m) at its highest point.*

46

Above *Twin marvels of engineering side by side: the Forth Bridges seen from the southern shore of the firth. Over 400,000 tons of concrete went to build the road bridge, on the left, with its 500ft (152m) towers, which was completed in 1964. The mile-long cantilevered railway bridge was finished in 1890 and it takes three years to paint it.*

Right *Scene in the tropical hothouses at Duthie Park in Aberdeen. The 'granite city' at the mouth of the River Dee is now the major Scottish base for North Sea oil and gas.*

Left *Main door of the Old University building in Aberdeen. The city has been an important port ever since the Middle Ages and the university, one of the oldest in Britain, was founded in 1495.*

Following spread *Cloud-capped Slioch – 'The Spear' – rises a sheer 3217ft (980m) in grandeur above the head of Loch Maree in the north-western Highlands. The loch is famous for salmon and sea-trout. Pilgrims used to make the arduous journey to an island in the loch where St Maree lived as a hermit in the 7th century.*

Scotland

Right *Scotland's second city, Glasgow, once renowned for ship-building, has built up a new reputation as a lively focus for culture with an enjoyable array of Victorian and Edwardian buildings. Here fireworks explode with suitable glitter above the Finnieston Shipyard.*

Below *Buchanan Street is Glasgow's smartest shopping street and Fraser's store preserves the look and atmosphere of a bygone and more elegant age.*

Above *The opulent Edwardian interior of Glasgow's King's Theatre, opened in 1904. Now run by the city council, it hosts professional and amateur productions and a Christmas pantomine.*

Right *The Scottish National Orchestra has its home base in Glasgow and rehearses in the Henry Wood Hall, a former church in Claremont Street. Scottish Opera and Scottish Ballet are also based in the city.*

Above *Glasgow is well supplied with parks. This is Victoria Park, dating from the 1880s and containing a grove of fossilized tree stumps 350 million years old.*

Left *Glasgow Cathedral is a severely plain building, dedicated to St Mungo (also known as Kentigern), who founded a church here in the 6th century in a 'green hollow', which is the meaning of the name Glasgow.*

Scotland

Previous spread *Scotland has 787 islands, of every variety of size and shape, some inhabited and others not. Most of them lie off the western and northern coasts. Benbecula is one of the Outer Hebrides, 6 miles (9½km) long, flat and full of water. This view looks south to the neighbouring island of South Uist.*

56

Above *Ruined Castle Moil stretches gaping fangs to the sky at Kyleakin on the Isle of Skye, where the ferries make the short crossing from the mainland. Originally constructed against marauding Norsemen, the castle was a stronghold of the Mackinnons of Strath in the Middle Ages.*

Left *A priest about to board the ferry from Mull across the sound to the diminutive and much venerated island of Iona. It was the burying place of the early kings of Scots and it was there that St Columba founded a monastery in the 6th century, from which missionaries went out to convert the mainland Scots and Picts to Christianity.*

Above *The black house at the Colbost Folk Museum in Skye is a typical low-slung crofter's home of the 19th century, built of stone with a turf roof. The family lived under the same roof with their farm animals for warmth and security.*

Scotland

Above *A prehistoric standing stone brings a touch of the sinister to peaceful countryside near Aridhglas in the south-west peninsula of Mull. Some 24 miles (38km) long by 26 miles (42km) across, Mull is the largest of the Inner Hebrides, with a 300-mile (483km) coastline of cliffs and sandy beaches.*

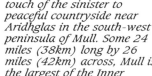

Left *Harris in the Outer Hebrides forms one island with Lewis, lying 35 miles (56km) or so off to the west of mainland Scotland. It gave its name to Harris tweed and is also known for fine knitwear. The tweeds were originally made for the islanders' own use, but commercial exploitation began in the 19th century.*

Left *Harris is celebrated for rugged scenery, sandy beaches and hordes of ferocious midges. The seaward views are magnificent and the sunsets unforgettable.*

61

Above *An elderly resident of the Isle of Lewis in the Outer Hebrides. 'The Gaelic', as it is honorifically called here, is still the first language of this remote outpost of Scotland, whose inhabitants are known for their old-world courtesy and for the strictness with which they keep the Sabbath.*

Left *The harbour at Malvaig, a small settlement on Loch Roag on the western coast of Lewis. Crofting and fishing remain the principal occupations of Lewis and Harris, the chief remaining bastion of traditional Scots Gaelic culture and way of life.*

Index

The page numbers in this index refer to the captions and not necessarily to the pictures accompanying them.

Acknowledgements

All the photographs in this publication are from The Automobile Association's photo library, with contributions from:

M Adelman, P & G Bowater, D Corrance, D Hardley, S & O Mathews, Stephan Gibson Photography, R Weir and H Williams with the exception of:

Front cover: Ronald Weir – Loch Alsh and Eilean Donan Castle.

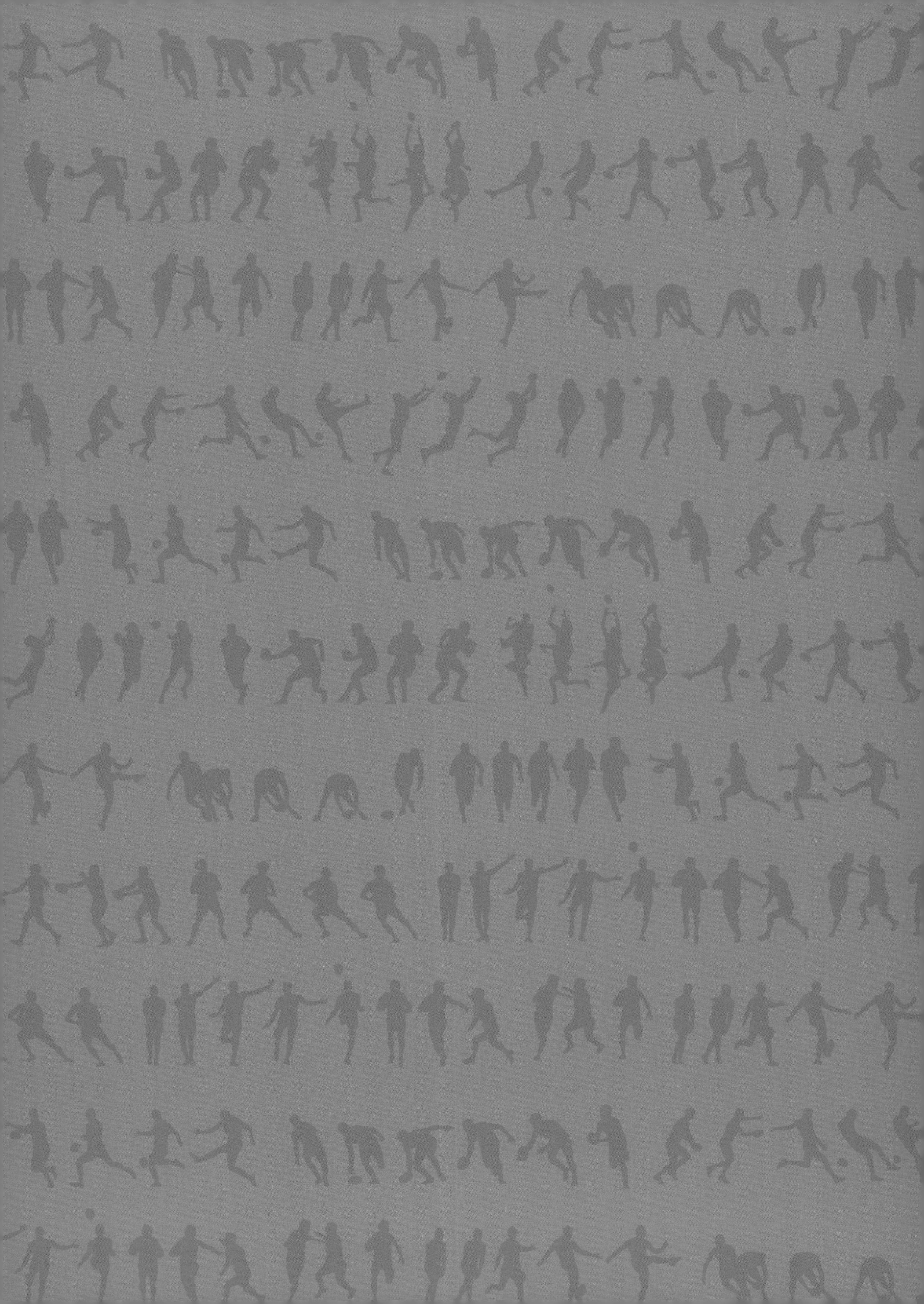

SKILLS
of Australian Football
Foreword by Denis Pagan

National Library of Australia Cataloguing-in-Publication entry
Kotton, Howard.
Skills of Australian Football
9780980597370 (hbk.)
Australian Football – Study and teaching.
796.336

® ™ The AFL logo and competing teams' logos, emblems and name of this product are all trade marks of and used under licence
from the owner, the Australian Football League, by whom all © copyright and other rights of reproduction are reserved.
Australian Football League, AFL House, 140 Harbour Esplanade, Docklands, VIC 3008

ISBN 978-0-9805973-7-0

The Slattery Media Group Pty Ltd
140 Harbour Esplanade, Docklands, VIC 3008
visit *slatterymedia.com*

Group publisher: Geoff Slattery Editor: Howard Kotton Sub-editor: Gary Hancock
Writers: Nick Bowen, Ben Collins, Peter Di Sisto, Michael Lovett, Peter Ryan, Andrew Wallace
Art director: Andrew Hutchison Deputy art director: Sam Russell Designer: Jarrod Witcombe
Photo editors: Natalie Boccassini, Melanie Tanusetiawan, Akane Utsunomiya Production manager: Troy Davis
Photography: The Slattery Media Group

Technical advice in this book has been provided by Lawrie Woodman and Jim Cail of the AFL Development Department.

COVER: Some of the most skilful stars in the game, clockwise from top, Richmond's Matthew Richardson, Fremantle's Matthew Pavlich
(pictured contesting with Port Adelaide's Alipate Carlile), Brisbane Lions' Jonathan Brown, Hawthorn's Sam Mitchell, Essendon's
Mark McVeigh, Geelong's Cameron Ling, Collingwood's Alan Didak, West Coast's Dean Cox and Adelaide's Brett Burton.

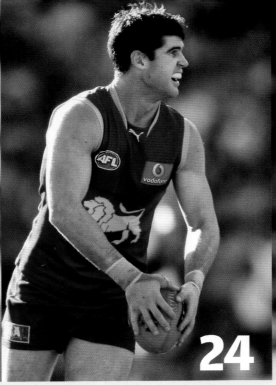

14 **24** **32**

SKILLS
of Australian Football

16

PLAY LIKE THE CHAMPIONS: Some of the AFL's biggest names analyse and explain the skills of the game. Clockwise from top left: Geelong's Steve Johnson, the Brisbane Lions' Jonathan Brown, West Coast's Dean Cox, Hawthorn's Sam Mitchell, Fremantle's Ryan Crowley, Adelaide's Tyson Edwards, Essendon's Matthew Lloyd and Port Adelaide's Daniel Motlop.

42

74 **88**

92

EXPERIENCED VOICE: Denis Pagan knows the value of hard work in a career spanning more than 30 years as a player and coach.

Foreword

By Denis Pagan

//// Two-time AFL premiership coach Denis Pagan believes mastering the basic skills of Australian Football is critical to success.

Success in football – and in life for that matter – requires planning, commitment, dedication, persistence and mental toughness over a long period of time. It is also about belief in yourself and a genuine desire, accepting that if you want something badly enough you can achieve it.

I have long believed that doing the basics (and some of the harder elements of the game) well over and over again is essentially what the game is about. By performing at a high level consistently at training and during games, a player earns the trust of his teammates and coaches, grows in confidence and continues to add value to his team.

My time in the game has taught me that there are some fundamentals that players must master to survive and prosper at the elite level. Players must have excellent disposal skills (especially effective kicking and handball), strong character, football smarts or IQ, courage and the ability to compete one-on-one and win his own ball.

Skills of Australian Football is a superb guide for players wanting to learn the fundamentals I have outlined, including kicking, marking and hand skills, as well as some of the more challenging components of the game including decision making, adapting to inclement weather, setting up at stoppages and a favourite of all coaches, 'one-percenters'. It also provides advice for coaches and umpires wanting to prepare for the game and improve their critical skills.

Based on interviews and technical advice from more than 30 AFL players and coaches and the AFL's technical coaching experts, *Skills of Australian Football* explains the importance of the fundamental skills, outlines how players go about executing those skills and lists some of the key teaching points designed to improve skill execution.

Often in analysing the game and the athletic feats we see from players on a regular basis, there is a tendency to categorise them as freaky or extraordinary. Having been involved in the game at the elite level as player and coach for more than 30 years, I can tell you that those who perform the freaky and extraordinary on a regular basis often are the players who work on their game harder and more diligently than most. They are probably blessed with natural talent, but they make the most of what they have been given by perfecting their skills, by doing the basics correctly.

I have always believed that the best coach for individual improvement is you. *Skills of Australian Football*, when used to complement a structured football training and preparation regime, will help you better understand how skills are executed and provide you with practical tips designed to improve all aspects of your game. I recommend *Skills of Australian Football* to anyone aiming to become as good as they can be.

Remember, by failing to prepare, you're preparing to fail. If you really want to be successful, the answer lies in total commitment. It's as simple as that.

DENIS PAGAN
Coach of North Melbourne premiership teams in 1996 and 1999 and coach of TAC Cup club Northern Knights.

THE PINNACLE: North Melbourne coach Denis Pagan and players celebrate winning the 1999 Grand Final.

ON TARGET: Carlton's Brendan Fevola is regarded as one of the best kicks for goal in the AFL. He is always well balanced, keeps his head over the ball and follows through.

Kicking skills

//// Kicking skills have improved immensely over the years as players have more time to practise and perfect hitting targets – or finding ways to kick "miracle" goals.

Of all the skills required to play Australian Football, kicking remains the most basic and, despite the proliferation of handball, it is still the favoured form of disposal.

There are many different types of kicks and several mechanics and skill sets are required to kick the ball – as outlined in the following pages – but at the end of the day, a kick is required to record the game's most important statistic: a goal.

In the modern game, it is crucial that field and goalkicking is mastered. Whereas many decades ago, it was common for players to either miss targets or kick the ball as long and as far as they could, today's player can't afford to "cough up" the ball to use the football vernacular.

Players not only spend more time practising their kicking drills today, they do so at game-pace, often simulating a match situation. It is vital that a player finds his target so that his teammate hardly has to change stride, particularly

so for a leading forward, who will more often than not have a defender breathing down his neck.

In the 1960s, it was not uncommon to see Geelong rover Bill Goggin burst out of the centre and deliver a bullet-like stab pass to the burly frame of full-forward Doug Wade. Collingwood had a similar combination with the highly skilled Barry Price regularly hitting his star full-forward Peter McKenna lace out.

Today we see players the calibre of Collingwood's Alan Didak spearing a pass to a leading teammate or Essendon's Mark McVeigh hitting a target with a perfectly weighted pass.

There are two other points of difference to how Didak and McVeigh deliver the ball today, compared with Goggin and Price of yesteryear.

First, a rule was introduced in 2002 that the ball must travel at least 15 metres (previously it was 10 metres) to be a mark. Second, today's player doesn't use the stab pass, or drop kick, which was consigned to the old highlight reels many years ago.

The most popular kick in Australian Football today is the drop punt, where the ball is released so the pointy end of the ball makes contact with the top part of the foot.

It is a safe choice endorsed by most players (and coaches) and is also the preferred choice when taking a set shot for goal, as outlined by Brisbane Lions sharpshooter Daniel Bradshaw.

The torpedo punt was also a popular kick decades ago but the need for players to pin-point teammates accurately further afield has meant it is employed less frequently.

However, it is often used for shots at goal from a long distance, usually after the siren has sounded to end a quarter or the game, and players such as Collingwood's Anthony Rocca can execute a torpedo punt to great effect.

Then there are the "trick" kicks such as the banana kick and snap shot, covered here by Port Adelaide's Daniel Motlop and Geelong's Steve Johnson respectively.

1 APPROACH
As he prepares to kick, Didak is balanced as he runs towards his target, with his weight on his kicking leg.

2 WIND UP
Didak takes a long last stride to help generate power, while the non-guiding (right) arm swings out and back for balance.

Field kicking

//// **Collingwood star Alan Didak is renowned as one of the best kicks in the AFL. He talks about why he is such a good kick and has some sound advice for football's next generation about the important art of kicking the ball.**

Alan Didak's ability to kick the football with uncanny accuracy and precision did not happen overnight. The talented Magpie honed his skills over many years of practice in the backyard and at school in South Australia.

As a youngster, Didak practised at every opportunity. "Most of the time I was kicking the footy with my mates," he said.

As Didak swings on to his trusty left foot, the hopes of the vast Magpie army are raised in expectation. Whether it's putting a drop punt down a teammate's throat or a miraculous snap from the boundary, he rarely lets them down.

In the heat of action every week, Didak says he does not have time to think about his kicking too much – he just does what comes naturally. "I honestly don't even think about it, I just do it. Hopefully it comes off," he said.

When he has time to go back behind the mark and kick the ball, Didak's major

3 IMPACT
He drops the ball vertically with his guiding hand as he is about to make contact with his boot. His support leg braces his body while the knee is tightly flexed before quickly extending for contact. The non-guiding hand comes forward, while his head is still over the ball.

4 FOLLOW THROUGH
Didak's leg accelerates through impact as his body drives forward and up. Contact is made high on his instep and he follows through towards the target with his head still.

priority is to ensure he is "nice and relaxed". "I just walk back and take a couple of deep breaths," he said. Didak prefers to use his left boot, although he admits he is kicking more on his non-preferred right these days.

Despite being one of the best kicks in the AFL, Didak continues to work hard on his kicking at training.

He has some advice for youngsters aspiring to kick as well as he does. "Make sure you get out there in a backyard or paddock and keep practising your technique," he said. "Make sure you hit the target and practise on both sides of the body. And make sure you're improving your kick because there's no point practising unless you're getting better."

A basic skill of Australian Football

Kicking is the most important skill in Australian Football. The basic skill of kicking should be taught at a young age and any faults rectified. It is important players learn the right technique while they are young.

Each week most AFL players demonstrate the ability to:

(a) kick under pressure;

(b) pass the ball accurately to a teammate; and

(c) use the ball to the best advantage of their side when kicking from a set position.

POINTS TO REMEMBER

1 Line up your body with the target. Have your head slightly bent over the ball. Hold the ball over the thigh of the kicking leg.

2 Guide the ball down with one hand.

3 Point your toes at your target – watch the ball hit the foot.

4 Follow through straight towards the target.

The preferred kick among AFL players is the drop punt. Other kicks include the torpedo punt, which is generally used for long distances.

Weighted kick

//// **Many AFL players have become expert at using the weighted kick to put their teammates into space and enable them to run on to an easy ball.**

As youngsters growing up on the NSW Central Coast, Essendon star Mark McVeigh and his brother, Sydney midfielder Jarrad, adopted a novel method of honing their kicking skills.

Their father Tony, who played with Williamstown in the Victorian Football Association, painted a target on the trampoline at their home in Terrigal which the brothers would take turns trying to hit. They would practise the weighted kick by leaving the trampoline in its usual spot and trying to lob the ball perfectly in the middle. When practising their passes, the trampoline would be slanted on an angle and they would aim to hit the middle of the target.

"Jarrad and I did that nearly every day when we were not at training and having a kick in the backyard," McVeigh said. "We would probably do that 100 times. That's just a childhood memory from the age of 10 until I moved out of home. I wasn't always a great kick and I worked very hard at it."

By the time he had reached his late teens and was drafted by Essendon, McVeigh realised he was a good exponent of the weighted kick.

"I felt comfortable on an AFL field and could hit most targets at a good rate," he said. "You develop the strength in your legs and you get a bit smarter with your footy."

McVeigh said the spot where the weighted kick was aimed to land depended on the situation and desired target.

"At times it is very much dictated by the player who is leading at you, the way he leads. I can use Matthew Lloyd as an example because I've kicked to him a number of times over a number of years. If he calls for it over the back, then I'm going to weight it over the back, so he can run on to it and give himself room from his opponent.

"If I think he has got a metre on his opponent, I'll sit it up, so he can run on to it. If a guy is right on his hammer, I'll change it up and deliver a 'worm-burner' straight into his hands, so the opponent has no chance of spoiling it.

"I speak to 'Lloydy' and Scott Lucas a fair bit. I know exactly how they like me to kick it to them. They both like it hard into their hands. They're both hard-leading forwards who come right at you. With James Hird, he was very good out in front but very good out the back, so often I'd weight them out the back to him."

McVeigh said it was harder to execute the weighted kick in windy conditions.

"You can still do it, but obviously you've got to allow for the wind," he said. "It makes it a bit trickier, because if you give it too much it's going to carry, but if you don't give it enough it's going to sit up and give your teammate's opponent a chance to spoil."

McVeigh said one of the best exponents of the weighted kick in his time in football was his former teammate Mark Mercuri.

"I always admired Mark Mercuri's kicking," he said. "There are so many good kicks in the AFL these days and some of the better ones are Hawthorn's Luke Hodge and Geelong's Josh Hunt. I wouldn't put myself in their category as a kick."

PRECISION: Hawthorn star Luke Hodge has also mastered the weighted kick.

TEACHING POINTS

1 The weighted kick uses the same kicking technique as the normal drop punt. But the aim is to give the kick more 'air time' and land it where a teammate is either already positioned or could run on to it.

2 The kick is not so much about power, but more about 'touch'. The player calling for the ball should be able to run to the position where the ball will land and mark it without losing momentum.

3 It is important players aim for a position on the ground to land the ball on.

JUST THE RIGHT WEIGHT:
Essendon's Mark McVeigh has
perfected the weighted kick
thanks to a unique training
drill using a trampoline in the
backyard of his family home.

1 **PREPARATION**
Bradshaw is facing directly towards the goal and has picked out a target through the goals. He starts his approach from well behind the mark, in a relaxed manner. He holds the ball with both hands evenly placed down the side of the ball and fingers comfortably spread.

2 **APPROACH**
He is accelerating his run-up in preparation to kick, continuing in a straight line towards the goals. He stays relaxed and avoids excessive movements of the ball, aligning it over his kicking leg in the last stride. To assist in keeping it still, the ball should be held over the kicking leg.

3 **RELEASE**
Bradshaw is watching the ball and has taken a typical long last stride before the kick, "leaving his kicking leg behind". His non-guiding (left) hand has come off the front of the ball and is swinging up and back to assist with balance. His right hand has stayed on the ball for as long as possible to control its path and positioning.

Goalkicking

//// Daniel Bradshaw is doing something right with his kicking for goal, shooting at almost 71 per cent in 2008. The veteran Brisbane Lions full-forward has a relaxed style and set routine, employing the drop punt to great effect.

A chat with club psychologist Phil Jauncey about eight years ago has had a positive effect on Daniel Bradshaw's mindset when kicking for goal.

In his early days with the Brisbane Lions, Bradshaw would go back, pull up his socks and think about the shot for a few seconds before walking in to kick. That changed after the chat with Jauncey.

"He said to me that with my personality I'm probably not somebody who should go back and think about it too much," Bradshaw said. "I just try to get back, take a couple of deep breaths, lean forward and pretty much get straight into it."

Bradshaw has a routine that he tries to follow and it worked for him in 2008, when he kicked 75.31.

"I work out where the mark is, so I get back far enough from that," Bradshaw said. "I go back about 15-20 metres, then I count six steps as I'm walking in and get a bit of momentum up.

4 **IMPACT**
Bradshaw's head is perfectly positioned over his support leg, which is firmly planted and bracing his body. His body is square to the goals and balanced and is driving forward and up into the kick. His ankle and foot are fully extended and stiff through impact and his toes are pointing towards the target.

5 **FOLLOW THROUGH**
He has watched the ball closely and his head has remained still. He has followed through fully, with his kicking leg continuing to extend towards the target. The follow through reflects what has gone into the kick and a poor one may result in inaccurate kicking, less distance or possibly injury.

"I have a bit of a jog in, so I've got my body going forward. I try to look at something through the goal, like someone's hat, and kick towards that.

"I'm probably more relaxed now. When you first start out, you get more nervous if you miss a couple of shots. Goalkicking is a bit fickle. Some weeks you might kick five or six straight, and the next week you might kick 1.5."

Bradshaw uses the drop punt and tries to kick the ball the same way, regardless of whether he is close to goal or a long way out.

"Sometimes when you're close in, you just try to poke it through and don't kick through the ball," he said. "I try to make

sure I've got my head over the ball and watch the footy right on to my boot."

Bradshaw said he did not do a lot of goalkicking at training.

"I don't overdo it," he said. "I might have five or six shots after training. I try to make sure the shots I do have go through."

Bradshaw was a keen Hawthorn supporter as a youngster and idolised champion spearhead Jason Dunstall. The Brisbane Lions full-forward was influenced by the goalkicking techniques of Dunstall and Geelong legend Gary Ablett Snr.

"They both had relaxed styles," Bradshaw said. "Growing up in the '80s,

ROUTINE THE KEY
Kicking for goal is one of the most important skills a footballer can master. If a player can have a consistent routine, this will help in his ability to kick successfully.

Jason Dunstall was my favourite player, and he had a pretty simple technique."

Among the better kicks for goal playing in the AFL today are Carlton spearhead Brendan Fevola and Essendon captain Matthew Lloyd. Fevola has the ability to kick goals from long distances, as well as boot remarkable snap goals from any angle. Lloyd is still most reliable from the set kick.

Snap kick for goal

//// Steve Johnson is a magician in front of the sticks. While he often makes the miraculous look easy, it has taken a lifetime of practice for the Geelong forward and 2007 Norm Smith medallist. Even today, he never stops practising.

Steve Johnson's sublime skills in front of goal are no accident. They are the result of hard work from the first time he picked up a football as a youngster in the Victorian town of Wangaratta.

Many have marvelled at the star Cat's ability to kick the miraculous goal and he continues to work on this talent, even after more than 100 games.

"It's something I've practised all my life, since I've kicked the footy when I was five years old," Johnson said. "When you go down to the park or the local footy ground with a group of mates, you don't go out to the front of the goals, you always go to the boundary line and try to kick the miracle goal. At quarter-time, half-time and three-quarter time of matches, you go out and have a few snaps at goal and try to kick a banana."

At training, Johnson tries to simulate match conditions when practising snap shots, so that it comes naturally in a game.

1 PREPARATION

Johnson is preparing to shoot from a tight angle near the boundary line and is using a snap kick. He is side on to the goals and the ball is held across the body, with the right hand forward and the other end of the ball pointing towards the target. He is looking at his focus point behind the centre of the goals.

2 APPROACH

He has opened up the target and gained momentum for the kick. He guides the ball down with his right hand so it will fall at an angle across his foot. His non-guiding arm is moving up and backwards off the ball for balance.

3 WIND UP

Johnson is in the classic wind-up position for all kicks, with a long last stride on to his support leg. He has his back extended, hip rotated back and extended and leg flexed behind. He is watching the point of contact on the ball throughout.

4 IMPACT

He kicks well in front of his body and has contacted the right end of the ball (away from the goals), producing a spin on the ball so that it curves through the air towards the centre of the goals.

5 FOLLOW THROUGH

The follow through continues in a straight line through the kick as the ball travels to the goals. This is the one instance when the follow through does not go directly towards the target. If it is a set kick, there will be time for only about two steps before the kick because the umpire will call play on as soon as he steps off the line.

"We do it under a lot of pressure, so when it comes to a game situation you can perform under pressure," he said. "When you're doing the warm-up, we're basically running around the boundary and what I try to do is have a footy in my hands when we're getting near the goals. If I get a spare 30 seconds when I'm not stretching, I like to have a few shots just for practice."

Johnson is an expert at the banana and the dribbling kick on the run from an acute angle, much like his hero as a youngster, Collingwood legend Peter Daicos.

"I used to love watching him (Daicos) do dribble kicks and all sorts of snap kicks. That's why I loved him as a player," Johnson said. "If you kick a dribble (goal) from the left-hand pocket, you want to kick a banana with your right foot. If you can get the ball dribbling end over end, you want to get the ball bouncing the first time a metre or two in front of you, so it starts in the right direction.

"A lot of the time people have the problem of trying to kick it about five metres in front of them. By that stage it loses the right sort of spin on the ball and it can dribble anywhere.

"When having a set shot from an angle, instead of pretending you're going to kick a drop punt and then kicking a snap, I find it's better to position yourself to kick the snap, so you're not under as much pressure.

HITTING THE TARGET

Snap kicks are generally used when shooting for goal from a tight angle or around the base of a pack such as in a stoppage in the forward 50, or crumbing near the goals.

"If I can get in the right position and take a couple of steps, I get square with the goals, put the ball in the right position in my hands, then drop it and make contact on the point and have a good follow through."

Johnson is one of many players who have thrilled fans with their ability to kick the impossible goal. Others include Carlton's Eddie Betts, Collingwood's Leon Davis and Hawthorn's Cyril Rioli.

Banana kick for goal

//// It is known in South Australia as the checkside and is most effective when kicking for goal from an acute angle. Classy Port Adelaide forward Daniel Motlop makes it look easy from either a set shot or on the run.

Port Adelaide sharpshooter Daniel Motlop prefers to use the banana, or checkside kick as it is called in South Australia, when he is forced on to his wrong (left) side.

"I'm just more comfortable with it," Motlop said. "I haven't used my left (foot) over the years and my first reaction is to checkside it. Other blokes would probably use their left foot."

Motlop started using the banana kick in games after watching former Geelong and Adelaide goalsneak Ronnie Burns employ it when caught on his wrong (right) foot.

The Power forward is confident using the kick on the run or from a set shot.

As a junior he did not use the kick much, but has found it more than useful under the pressures of AFL football.

Early in his career when he was at North Melbourne, he would practise the kick with teammate Daniel Wells. "You practise your checksides from the right-hand forward pocket with set shots," Motlop said.

1 APPROACH
Holding the ball in the classic "reverse torpedo" grip, Motlop has started his run-up from tight on the boundary and moves to open up the goals on his right. As in all kicks, he keeps his head still and watches the ball throughout.

2 GUIDE DOWN
During the second last step he has started to guide the ball down with his right hand, so that it drops at an angle across the foot. His left hand is looping up and back from the ball.

3 BRACE
The ball is falling at an angle across his body towards the impact area. He begins to brace with his support leg as the flexed right knee is accelerating towards the contact point.

4 IMPACT
While bracing on his left leg as the ball drops towards impact, Motlop accelerates his kicking foot towards the ball and makes contact under the left end of the ball.

5 FOLLOW THROUGH
The kicking foot follows through in a straight line (not towards the target in this case) as the ball begins to spin rapidly sideways which makes it curve in flight towards the target.

He has kicked several superb goals with the banana kick, including a memorable one from the boundary line from outside 50m against the Brisbane Lions at the Gabba in 2007.

Motlop said that goal had an element of luck about it and it was easier to control the banana when he dribbled the ball along the ground.

He said using the banana kick along the ground in wet conditions required a different mindset as the ball would not roll back as far, meaning you had to kick it straighter.

Motlop said one of the better exponents in the AFL was speedy Collingwood rover Leon Davis.

"He always does them and never misses," Motlop said.

Port Adelaide coach Mark Williams has enough confidence in the forward to give him the freedom to make the right decision on which kick he uses in matches.

"He's OK. It's not as if I try to go out and do it every game," Motlop said.

"It's just a spur of the moment thing. A couple of times it's come off pretty well.

"You live and die by the sword a bit. If it comes off, it's all good, but if it doesn't, your teammates can have a crack at you.

"A couple of my better goals have come from a checkside kick. It's working for me, so I'll stick to it."

THE GRIP: The ball is held like a reverse torpedo punt, with the right hand forward for a right-foot kick.

1 RUN-UP
Rocca holds the ball with the torpedo grip during his six-step run-up. He brings the ball up with both hands to the position from which he will guide the ball down. His head is still and he is watching the ball throughout the kick.

2 GUIDE DOWN
He guides the ball down in line with his kicking leg with the same hand as his kicking foot. The ball is guided down at the same angle as it is held in the grip. His non-guiding hand is swinging up and back in a loop from the front of the ball for balance.

3 BRACE
He is releasing the ball during the longer last stride (to increase power). The knee of his kicking leg is flexed to allow a quick and strong extension of the leg and acceleration of the foot into the kick. His non-guiding arm is swinging through in line with his kicking leg.

Torpedo punt

//// It is not used as often these days, but the torpedo can be most effective when kicking for distance. One of the best exponents is Collingwood's Anthony Rocca, who has the ability to lift his team and the crowd with his trusty right boot.

Anthony Rocca is one of the most consistently long kicks in the AFL and enjoys the feeling when he hits the sweet spot with the torpedo punt.

"If it goes the right way and it goes where you want it, and if it goes through for a goal, it can be very lifting individually and team-lifting as well," Rocca said. "It can get the crowd up too."

Rocca said the best time to use the torpedo was at the end of quarters when all teammates were covered and there were no options to give the ball off from outside the 50m arc.

Rocca would often kick the torpedo in the backyard with his big brother Sav. "I used to kick torpedos for fun, but now it is a pretty rare kick in the AFL," he said.

"We don't really practise it a lot. Every now and then, you probably have a couple of shots after training."

Rocca uses about six steps before he launches into the torpedo. "All you need is

4 IMPACT
Rocca's support leg is acting as a brace to transfer momentum from his body to his kicking leg. His body drives forward and up from his support leg and his kicking leg accelerates through the point of impact with the ball. His head remains still.

5 FOLLOW THROUGH
After his kicking foot has accelerated through the point of impact, it continues in a straight line towards the target.

a little bit of momentum," he said. "If you get the right technique, the ball can really fly off."

Rocca believes the torpedo can be more effective than other kicks in wet conditions. "The ball is a bit heavier, so it's not going to move around a lot in your hands," he said. "If you get the right technique going, you kick it a bit longer than a normal drop punt."

But the torpedo becomes problematic in windy conditions, with Rocca preferring to use the drop punt into a breeze.

"It's pretty hard against the breeze because trying to get the ball from hand to foot is really important with a torpedo," Rocca said. "If you've got the breeze, you

kick the ball longer and better if you think about the technique of it.

"If you're going for distance and trying to kick the leather off the football, most of the time you find that it comes off the wrong way and goes off the side of the boot. It is very rare that you get the sweet spot when you're trying to kick it too hard."

He would love to see the torpedo used more often in matches, but recognises its popularity has diminished in the modern game.

"It is a team game and you've got to look at using the ball and finding better options," he said. "But when the torpedo is done well, it comes off pretty well."

THE GRIP: The ball is held on an angle across the body.

IN SAFE HANDS:
St Kilda star Nick Riewoldt
takes more than his share
of marks, usually on his
chest as shown here.

02
Marking skills

//// Whether it is the safe chest mark or the high-flying variety, the mark is one of the unique features of our game and requires great judgment and often plenty of courage.

Few facets of Australian Football have such varying degrees of difficulty as the mark. There is the safe option (the chest mark), the tougher variety (the hand mark) and the most spectacular of all (the hanger).

But there is no doubt it's the latter which brings fans to their feet and raises the decibel level of commentators as it seems every year we are treated to a feast of high-flying aerialists.

Today, there are only old black and white photographs but how we'd love to see clear and colourful vision of greats such as South Melbourne's Bob Pratt soaring through the air on a regular basis.

Taking marks as Pratt required tremendous skill and judgment, not to mention courage, and he was one of the pioneers of the spectacular mark during the 1930s.

A decade or so later, Essendon's John Coleman became the poster-boy of Australian Football as he thrilled fans with his high-flying; through the

1960s and 1970s it was Carlton's Alex Jesaulenko while flamboyant Sydney full-forward Warwick Capper grabbed attention as much for his high marks as for his tight shorts in the 1980s. Around that time, Richmond's Michael Roach and Fitzroy's Alastair Lynch were captured in all their glory on film as they took their respective marks of the year.

Grand Final day has also been saved for some of the most spectacular – and important – marks the game has seen.

One of the first to grace the television screens was Richmond tyro Royce Hart gliding across an opponent to take a crucial mark late in the 1967 Grand Final against Geelong.

Jesaulenko produced the most famous in the 1970 Grand Final between Carlton and Collingwood. The call of television commentator Mike Williamson – "Jesaulenko, you beauty!" – remains one of the most celebrated in football history.

North Melbourne spearhead Phil Baker unleashed a series of incredible marks in the 1978 Grand Final against

Hawthorn while, at the other end of the ground, fans were treated to the high-flying feats of Hawks star Peter Knights.

In more recent times, Sydney defender Leo Barry took what some have described as the most important mark in a Grand Final when he held on to a contested grab in the dying seconds of the 2005 Grand Final as the Swans held a slender lead.

Adelaide's Brett Burton is known as the 'Birdman' and that is an apt moniker given he is a regular mark of the year contender. On the following pages, the Crows forward gives his thoughts on how to take a hanger.

The safest marking option is the chest mark and players with the physical attributes of star Brisbane Lions forward Jonathan Brown can be difficult to stop on a lead.

The hand mark is usually taken by a leading forward and there has been no better exponent of the hand mark than Richmond's Matthew Richardson. Brown and Richardson share their views on their area of marking expertise.

Hand mark

//// Matthew Richardson has established a reputation as one of the best marks in the AFL. He is so hard to beat when he takes the ball out in front, a trait he learned watching some of the game's stars of the 1980s and early '90s.

As a budding footballer growing up in Tasmania, Matthew Richardson was encouraged to mark the ball with his hands out in front.

"The defender has less chance of being able to punch it away," Richardson said. "If you let the ball come into your chest, he's got a much better chance of punching it away. So I guess the idea is to keep the ball as far away from the defender as you can."

A teenage Richardson would be transfixed in front of the TV, admiring the sublime marking skills of Carlton premiership captain Stephen Kernahan and former St Kilda star Stewart Loewe.

It wasn't long before he was able to view them at close quarters when he joined the Tigers in 1993.

"His (Kernahan's) hands were pretty sticky. Once the ball went in, it didn't come out very often," Richardson said. Another player who caught Richardson's

1 EYES FOCUSED
Richardson has his body in a direct line with the flight of the ball. His eyes are focused on the ball and, with extended arms, he is in a good position to reach the ball before an opponent attempts to spoil. His fingers are outstretched, pointing upwards in the 'W' position.

2 FIRM GRIP
Richardson takes the ball in his hands in front of his eyes. He grips the ball firmly in his fingers and flexes his elbows slightly to absorb some of the force from the ball and provide greater control.

3 THE MARK
Having secured the ball, Richardson starts to pull it down towards his chest to protect it. His eyes have remained focused on the ball as he takes the mark.

attention with his marking was North Melbourne superstar Wayne Carey.

The way the game is played these days, there are fewer one-on-one marking contests and opportunities to take a pack mark. The rule preventing players chopping the arms of an opponent in a marking contest makes it imperative that those attempting to mark take the ball out in front as often as possible.

"The umpires are so harsh on any contact with your arms," Richardson said. "As a forward, if you try to take the ball out in your hands and your arms are fully stretched, the defender hasn't got much hope other than to chop your arms and then you're going to get a free kick.

"We're loath to kick to contests as much now, so you don't see as much pack marking. Footballers are probably a lot smarter.

"The backmen read the play so well and they zone off and come third man in, so you don't get as many one-on-one opportunities."

Marking the ball out in front when it is wet and slippery is much harder than in dry conditions and Richardson tailors his technique to suit.

"It's a lot harder to take one-grab marks in the wet," he said. "When it's wet, you lose a little bit of confidence. You probably try to start taking more chest marks in the wet.

"James Hird was pretty good at it – flatten your hands out, tap it once out in front of you and try to take it on the second grab."

Richardson practises his marking at every training session, always trying to take the ball in his hands. He advises avoiding taking chest marks at training.

"We probably get the marking bag out once a week, jump on that and practise our overhead marking," he said.

"You're always marking the ball in your normal drills. You're doing it every day. You're getting blokes to kick balls into your hands from short distances, longer distances, putting them up in the air."

1 APPROACH
Brown sprints on the lead straight towards the kicker and watches the ball intently as his body moves directly in line with the flight of the ball.

2 PREPARATION
As Brown reaches the last two steps towards the ball, he brings his arms up in preparation to take the mark. Note his hands and forearms are ready to go under the ball.

Chest mark

//// Jonathan Brown is hard to shift in a marking contest. With his imposing physique and strength, he is one of the best chest marks in the AFL. The Brisbane Lions star explains the finer side of one of the game's most important skills.

A man has got to know his limitations, Clint Eastwood told us in that immortal line from the smash-hit movie *Magnum Force* in 1973. That is certainly true of Brisbane Lions champion Jonathan Brown.

Brown knew from a young age that he did not have the blistering speed of Peter Matera or the leap of Warwick Capper. His greatest assets were his size and strength. He admired North Melbourne legend

Wayne Carey's ability to outmanoeuvre his opponent in a one-on-one contest and take the mark on his chest.

"For a lot of us younger guys coming through watching footy in the '90s, if you're a strong type of player, you certainly took a leaf out of Wayne's book. That was one of his many strengths," Brown said.

"I'm not the quickest player or have the biggest jump in the world. I've always worked pretty hard on the contested marking situation from a young age. Once

3 DROPPING DOWN
As the ball gets close to his body, Brown continues to move forward while dropping down to ensure the ball will be taken at chest height. His fingers and hands are extended with palms up and his elbows are beginning to tuck into the side.

4 THE MARK
Brown takes the ball in his hands and forearms and guides it into his chest. The mark is completed by hugging the ball tightly to his chest with his elbows tucked in to ensure that the mark cannot be spoiled.

I got to this level, I worked hard on the weights in the gym to make sure I had the strength to compete with the key defenders in the competition.

"That is hard early in your career when you don't have that physical development, but obviously now I'm in the prime of my physical development.

"With that comes more traffic around you and more guys trying to get back on top of you, so the one thing I have noticed is that it is becoming harder to get into the one-on-one situation."

In his early years, Brown tried to emulate the exploits of former teammate Alastair Lynch, whose strength in the contested situation was a feature of his game.

He also worked hard at training with former teammates Justin Leppitsch and Mal Michael and these days continues to practise hard with full-back Daniel Merrett.

"Once a week we try to work on our one-on-one contested marks with one of the defenders," the Lions captain said. "There will be a lot of contested marking situations, marking in your hands and on your chest."

As a youngster growing up in Warrnambool in country Victoria, Brown often played in wet conditions on muddy grounds where, not surprisingly, he found the chest mark was a better and far safer option.

But he prefers to take a mark out in front of his opponent with his hands.

"It is preferable to mark it in your hands for two reasons – the ball would be further away from the defender's fist if he is trying to spoil because you take it at a higher point. If you mark it in your hands, it also makes it easier to dish it off for the handball," Brown said.

Carey's ability to take marks running with the flight of the ball was legendary and Brown has emulated the feats of the former North Melbourne champion. In 2002, Brown was awarded the AFL Mark of the Year when he took a courageous mark running with the flight of the ball against Hawthorn at the MCG.

The hanger

//// Who better to advise on how to take a 'speccie' than 'The Birdman', Adelaide's Brett Burton. Timing is the key to how this Crow flies.

Brett Burton has always loved flying for 'speccies' but as a junior his coaches encouraged him to stay down and crumb. Ironically, Burton has since become so well known for his high-flying marks after making his debut for the Crows in 1999 that he is now almost universally known as 'The Birdman'.

Burton says it was not until a growth spurt in his late teens that he literally started to take off.

"When I was growing up I was quite small, I was 172cm until I was about 19," Burton said. "So all of my coaches throughout my juniors would encourage me to stay down and crumb."

Unperturbed, Burton continued to practise his high marking in kick-to-kick sessions at school and by himself at home, where he spent countless hours, kicking the ball high in the air and launching himself at it, always trying to take it at its highest point.

Burton's practice eventually paid off. After a growth spurt took him close to his current height of 185cm, Burton broke into Glenelg's SANFL team at 19 in 1998. Playing at centre half-forward, he finally had a licence to fly for his marks and The Birdman was hatched.

Drafted by the Crows at the end of that season, Burton brought his one-man air show to the AFL.

Much to the delight of crowds across the country, his three coaches at Adelaide – Malcolm Blight, Gary Ayres and Neil Craig – gave him free rein to continue doing what he does best.

Burton says high marking has become almost second nature to him, so much so he rarely practises it. "It certainly comes naturally to me now and you're best to stop thinking about it too much and just letting it flow," he said.

"For me, it's really all about the timing. What I tell myself is when you see the ball, hold yourself back, then go late and try to take the ball at its highest point.

"When I go for a mark, I don't necessarily try to take the biggest mark or a screamer.

"I always just watch the ball and try to take it at its highest point. I don't take any notice of anyone around me because you can't affect what they're going to do, you can't tell them to stay put so you can jump on them."

Even after turning 30, Burton continued to rack up the frequent flyer points, as evidenced by his classic hanger over Melbourne's Matthew Warnock in round eight, 2008.

"For me, the hanger is one of the reasons you play footy," the Crows veteran said. "It is exhilarating, you get a big buzz out of it. You can hear the crowd noise when you go up and, if you take it, it gets even louder.

"But it's not just from an individual point of view. When you see guys take hangers, it lifts the whole side. That's a good feeling to be able to lift your side."

Burton is not the only high-flyer in the AFL. Other players who regularly take a hanger include Melbourne's Russell Robertson, Collingwood's Dale Thomas, Essendon's Patrick Ryder and Fremantle's Luke McPharlin.

1 THE JUMP
Burton runs in to bring his body in direct line with the flight of the ball. His eyes are focused firmly on the ball and he has jumped powerfully off his take-off (left) leg to launch himself towards the ball.

2 THE SIT
On making contact with his opponent with his legs, Burton is extending them to push his body upwards to gain extra height. He is moving into perfect position to take the ball as high as he can.

3 EYES FOCUSED
With his eyes still firmly focused on the ball and head still, he has brought his hands together in the classical "W" position with thumbs almost touching and fingers outstretched. His arms are extended towards the ball.

4 THE MARK
He has taken the ball slightly in front of his face with arms extended and has flexed slightly at the elbows to absorb the force of the ball as it is firmly gripped with the fingers. He has started to pull the ball down to his chest.

BRILLIANT BULLDOG:
Adam Cooney used his hand
skills to great effect in 2008,
winning the Brownlow Medal.

03
Hand skills

//// **With greater emphasis on the running game, the use of the hands in a variety of skills is pivotal to setting up play and turning defence into attack.**

It could be argued that of all the football "body parts", the hand is the most important. After all, without first using your hands, you are not going to be able to perform the game's most basic skill - kicking.

While you will often hear recruiters talk up a potential player as having "quick hands", there is more to using your hands than firing out a handball at rapid pace.

Hand skills are crucial in so many areas of Australian Football. This includes ruck play, picking up the ball, tackling and bouncing the ball on the run. Each of those skills is covered in this section.

But of all the hand skills in the modern game, handball is the one component that can set the benchmark for a successful side.

And, unlike some players who might have a poor kicking technique, there is no excuse for being a poor exponent of the handball, given it is not an overly complicated process.

Handball has been used as an effective attacking - and defensive -

weapon since the 1970s. Before then, players were generally ordered to handball only if they were in trouble and never in defence.

But during the 1960s that started to gradually change, first with the arrival of Graham 'Polly' Farmer, a star ruckman from Western Australia who took the football world by storm when he joined Geelong in 1962.

Old black and white vision shows Farmer regularly firing 20-metre handballs to his teammates as the Cats became one of the most attacking sides of their era.

It's part of football folklore that at half-time in the 1970 Grand Final, Carlton coach Ron Barassi implored his players to handball at all costs as the Blues faced a 44-point deficit against Collingwood. History shows the Blues carried out their coach's instructions and claimed a memorable victory.

Len Smith, who coached a small Fitzroy team in the late 1950s and early 1960s, was an advocate of using handball but even he would be amazed

to learn today that some sides record more handballs than kicks.

In the modern game, Geelong midfielder Cameron Ling might not be the fastest player but he certainly possesses "quick hands" and he is well qualified to pass on the finer points of handball.

Every big man will argue that the ruckman is the most important player on the ground and history tells us that a dominant ruckman can set up his side. West Coast's Dean Cox is the pre-eminent ruckman of the modern era and he discusses the art of ruckwork.

Brisbane Lions midfielder Luke Power is a master of the one-handed pick-up - another important hand skill - while the running bounce is a great spectacle when properly executed. Geelong's Gary Ablett certainly knows how to weave and dodge his way past opponents.

Tackling is such an important facet and the Swans have excelled in this area in recent seasons. Sydney midfielder Jude Bolton explains the best way to lay a tackle.

Handball

//// Ever wondered why Geelong star Cameron Ling is so quick and sure with his hands? Here he says it is all about practice, practice and more practice.

It is hard to believe Cameron Ling is a right-hander because he is so proficient on his non-preferred side when he handballs. This is the result of years of practice in the backyard with his father Linton and brother David in Geelong.

"During my teenage years, I made sure I learned how to handball both hands and kick both feet," Ling said. "No matter how bad I was when I was younger, I used to handball on my left hand and get better and better at it – same with my right foot.

"When I moved into under-13s, under-15s and under-18s, it was more about doing everything as quick as I could. I tried to train myself under a bit of intensity, as if you were in a game.

"I think dad was the one I kicked the footy with the most. I mucked around with my brother a bit in the backyard. It was just that general ball skills."

As a midfielder often winning the ball in contested situations, Ling said handball was an important part of his game and he spent plenty of time practising his skills each week.

"I do a lot of close-in, quick hands sort of stuff, as well as flicking up ground balls to someone running past," he said. "We do indoor touch sessions, which involve a lot of handball and having to dish the ball off quickly off rebound nets.

"You've got to be able to take the ball cleanly in your hands and dish it off with a quick handball to a teammate.

"We practise the technique about how you gather the ball and protect yourself, so that you can turn and give the ball off

and hit the target. We do work where you hit the longer handball target."

When Ling takes possession, he makes a quick assessment of whether to kick or handball.

"If I'm in a position where I've got time and where I've got someone down the field, I'll always kick. If I'm in a contested situation and I'm about to be tackled and there's a teammate in a bit of space who can run and carry, I'll give the ball to him," he said.

ATTACKING WEAPON

In today's modern game, handball is a major attacking weapon as players run the ball from defence into attack. It is a skill that needs to be practised regularly and, by watching great handball exponents such as **Cameron Ling**, **Sam Mitchell** and **Daniel Cross**, you can improve your game.

TEACHING POINTS

1. The ball must be gripped lightly with the platform hand and hit with a clenched fist.

2. The punching fist is formed by placing the thumb outside, not inside, the fingers.

3. The stance is nearly side-on to allow the punching arm to swing through freely. Knees are slightly bent to maintain balance.

4. For a right-handed handball, the left foot is forward and vice versa for a left-handed handball.

5. The punching arm is also slightly bent.

1 POSITIONING
Ling is well balanced, with his body in a side-on position His weight is moving forward over his right leg and his eyes are focused on the target. Both arms are slightly bent and the ball is pointing towards the target. The fist of the punching hand is driving towards the end of the ball.

2 **IMPACT**
The eyes are still focused on the receiver and his weight is continuing to move forward. The striking fist has sent the ball in a direct line towards the target with some backspin (similar to a drop punt kick).

3 **FOLLOW THROUGH**
The punching hand continues to follow through towards the target and the stable head position has been maintained throughout. Ling is continuing to run on to follow up the handball and support the receiver.

Ruckwork

//// Star West Coast Eagle Dean Cox discusses the finer points of ruck play and says his goal is to palm the ball directly to a running teammate.

As Dean Cox prepares for a ruck contest at stoppages and boundary throw-ins, the star West Coast Eagle's major priority is to be in front of his opponent.

Cox says that taking the front position gives him more control over where to direct his hit-out. But his strategy at centre bounces can vary, depending on the tactics employed by the opposition.

"Being in front makes it a lot more difficult for the opposition ruckman to get a clean hit on the football," he said. "In the centre, it varies. You might have some players who might jump early or might come from different angles.

"It helps to mix it up with a different run-up or angle, so you don't become so predictable."

The four-time All-Australian ruckman spends plenty of time during the week at training working on set-ups with his midfielders. He prefers to palm the ball to a running teammate rather than hit it in an open space, which provides a greater risk of turning it over.

"At times there is a call for smacking the ball out into space, but with the amount of work we put into set-ups we want to target players," Cox said. "We want to block, so they can have a free run at the footy.

"If you just smash it forward, the chances are that it could end up in the opposition's hands.

"If you're down late in games, you can smash it forward, and if there's loads of space you can change it up, but I'd rather palm it."

CREATING THE PLAY

The role of the ruckman is crucial in setting up play from a variety of contests such as the centre bounce or boundary throw-in. To create opportunities for his smaller, running players, it is important that a ruckman has the skill to direct the ball to his teammates' best advantage. West Coast Eagles' **Dean Cox** and Port Adelaide's **Brendon Lade** are great exponents of ruck skills.

Cox is rarely flustered on the field, but is not happy when his hit-out is sharked by the opposing midfielders.

"I get stuck into my midfielders, just like they would do if I'm not getting my hands on the football," he said. "My role is to tap it to a certain area and their role is to get there."

As a young ruckman, Cox picked up plenty of tips from former teammate Michael Gardiner, as well as other experienced ruckmen including Matthew Primus, Steven King and Luke Darcy.

"I suppose I wasn't as strong as them and I tried to learn from a very young age the way they got in the best body position," Cox said.

"Once my strength came, I'd get in the right position and be able to tap it down to our midfield."

As a youngster growing up in Dampier, Western Australia, Cox played three years of basketball at high school, which he believes helped him with his development.

"When I came back to football, I was hungry to learn to play the game," he said.

1 THE LEAP
Following his run-up, Cox leaps towards the ball from one foot and swings both arms up to gain height. He watches the ball and prepares to palm it with his right hand to the space in front of his receiver. His body is side-on to his opponent for protection.

2 **PERFECT TIMING**
He times his leap to reach maximum height at the point where he will contact the ball. His palming arm is straight and his fingers are spread to get maximum control of the ball on contact. His eyes are focused on the ball and his left arm moves in a natural balancing action.

3 **DIRECTION**
He hits the ball with his open hand and firm fingers. The ball is directed towards the target and he follows through with his arm in the direction of the tap. By leaping to meet the ball at his maximum height, he beats his opponent to the ball and taps it cleanly before contact has occurred.

4 **THE BLOCK**
He follows through towards his target and contact by his opponent has no effect on the direction of the ball. He is in a good position to block his opponent from further involvement in the play and to take possession himself if the ball goes to ground.

One-handed pick-up

//// Brisbane Lions veteran Luke Power has some tips on picking up the footy, particularly when to go with one hand and when to go with two.

Two hands for beginners – that's Brisbane Lions vice-captain Luke Power's simple advice when picking up the footy. But there are times in a game when the sure ball handler prefers the one-handed pick-up.

"If the ball is lying still, it's probably quicker to pick it up with one hand," Power said. "But if the ball is rolling at pace, it's difficult to pick it up with one hand, so you've probably got to go with two hands.

"It depends if it's rolling towards you or away from you. If it's rolling away, you generally would pick it up with two hands.

"Basically, you've got to keep your eyes on the ball and keep your head as close to it as possible. If your head is further away, it is difficult to take the ball at one-touch."

Power estimated he would spend about two hours a week practising his ground-ball skills.

"I'm small, so I'm not going to be getting too much of my footy in the air," the 179cm midfielder said. "I'd probably spend a couple of hours a week picking up ground balls at training."

Power said players worked on their one-handed and two-handed pick-ups at training.

"I think players are so skilful now that they're able to do more things," he said. "I think players practise different skills now because the game is a lot quicker and you've got less time."

Power said young players should handle the ball as often as they can.

TAKING THE BALL

A one-handed pick-up is normally used only when the ball is still or moving slowly. A two-handed pick-up is always safest in ensuring clean possession and is critical if the ball is moving, which is usually the case during a game.

"As a kid, I think you should be practising everything," he said. "When you're a kid, it's not even practice, it's just fun. You'll be kicking the ball along the ground and picking it up as much as possible."

Playing on pristine surfaces such as the MCG, Telstra Dome and the Gabba makes it easier to pick up the ball. It's certainly a far cry from the days when players were wallowing in ankle deep mud on suburban grounds in Melbourne.

"We don't play on a bad surface now, all the surfaces are really, really good," he said. "It means the bounce of the ball is very honest."

Power, a triple premiership player and All-Australian, has played alongside some of the best ball handlers in the competition, including Brownlow medallists Michael Voss, Simon Black and Jason Akermanis.

One player who has caught his eye with his elite ball-handling skills is Adelaide forward Jason Porplyzia. Power rates the star Crow the best one-touch player in the AFL. "It's a pretty big wrap on a young bloke," the classy left-footer said. "He never fumbles and is very good below his knees."

1 **APPROACH**
Power is focused on the ball as he runs towards it. He approaches the ball to one side to allow him to reach for it comfortably with his right hand. He is about to plant his right foot close to the ball and is beginning to lower his body to initiate the pick-up.

2 CROUCH
He plants his right foot slightly behind and to the side of the ball, bends his right knee and lowers his right arm. His palm is open with his fingers pointing down and slightly spread, ready to go under the ball. He keeps his body close to the ball and his head over it.

3 SCOOP
The crouched Power scoops his right hand underneath the ball. While his right foot remains planted, his left leg continues to move forward. As his right hand reaches for the ball, his left arm extends up and outwards to help his balance.

4 COMING UP
Staying focused on the ball and coming up from his crouched position, Power brings the ball up with his right hand while bringing his left hand across to ensure a strong hold.

5 POSSESSION
Power grabs the football with both hands and is now able to lift his head and look for options. He carries the ball, ready to deliver by hand or foot. He is looking up the field for attacking options.

Tackling

//// **When it comes to tackling, Sydney has some of the best. Jude Bolton says the key to success is to focus on the hips.**

When Sydney star Jude Bolton is about to lay a tackle, his major focus is on his opponent's hips.

"You try to look for the hips. That's the base, that's where you know they'll be moving from," Bolton said. "If you take your focus off the hips, you can sometimes be (side-)stepped."

Bolton was renowned as a fine tackler before he joined Sydney from TAC Cup team Calder Cannons in 1999.

The blond Swan laid the third-most tackles in the League in 2008 with 142. Only teammate Brett Kirk (151) and St Kilda midfielder Lenny Hayes (143) made more.

Two of Bolton's younger teammates, Kieren Jack and Paul Bevan, come from rugby league backgrounds and the hard-working midfielder marvels at their tackling skills.

"They go at a million miles an hour in their desire to make the tackle," Bolton said. "They've got the league background and that's helped them. We get a lot of training from some of the union and league coaches.

"Our tackling coach Les Kiss has done a lot of work with us in terms of tackling from behind. You have to be able to twist them, turn them and roll with them, so you're not just charging in and giving away a free kick.

"For me, a lot of tackling is intent. Technique might take about 20 per cent of it and intent takes up the rest, in terms of just the desire to make that tackle and

KEYS TO GOOD TACKLING

Tackling takes practice, appropriate supervision and good coaching. There are three angles from which players can tackle – front, side and behind. Think of all the good tacklers in Australian Football and the first thing you realise is that they want to tackle when they know they can't win the ball or an opponent has the ball. The essence to good tackling, like all team play, is to want to do it and know how to do it.

make it stick. The technique is really your icing on the cake."

Bolton has played more than 200 games and says tackling skills have become more important in the AFL recently. "I think it's definitely stepped up another level," he said.

"I just want to make sure I'm not missing too many tackles, so that you're giving your teammates the best opportunity of winning the ball back."

Interestingly, the statistics back both Bolton and Kirk as two of the best tacklers of the past couple of years while the Swans have consistently been among the best tackling sides in the competition.

Since 1981 and to the end of the 2008 season, Kirk is the second best tackler in the AFL (991 in 195 games) while Bolton had laid 836 in 211 games to be seventh in that time-span. Former Bulldog Tony Liberatore leads with 1234 in 283 games.

In 2008, the Swans were the second-best tackling side in the AFL behind Geelong.

1 **EYES FOCUSED**
Bolton has his eyes focused on the hips of the opponent (Geelong's **Jimmy Bartel**) carrying the ball and is going in low to make the tackle. As Bartel is turning to evade the tackle, Bolton has gripped his body at waist level with his right hand.

2 **LOW AND STRONG**
Staying low to ensure that the tackle is made at the correct height (around the waist), Bolton's left arm is moving to wrap around Bartel's body and left arm which is controlling the ball. Bolton says that when he is about to tackle, his major focus is on his opponent's hips.

3 **ARMS PINNED**
Bolton has pinned Bartel's left elbow and is using both arms to pull his opponent strongly into his body and is beginning to drop his weight to drag his opponent down. The effect of the tackle has caused Bartel to begin losing control of the ball as he hurriedly attempts to handball.

4 **FREE BALL**
The tackle has caused the ball to spill free, giving Bolton or a teammate an opportunity to take possession and create a turnover. (If the player is judged to have had prior opportunity, a free kick would result for not immediately disposing of the ball with a kick or handball when tackled correctly).

Running bounce

//// Gary Ablett loves running and bouncing the ball when given the opportunity. But he says before you do it you have to be aware of who is around you.

There are few better sights in football than Geelong star Gary Ablett in full flight, bouncing the ball on his way towards goal.

Before he attempts a bounce, Ablett makes himself aware of the traffic around him, reducing the chances of being tackled.

"It's important that you have a quick glance up and know what's going on around you," the Cats champion said. "Bouncing takes only one or two seconds, so if you can see you're not going to be tackled, then it gives you time to take your bounce."

Ablett watches closely as he makes his first bounce, ensuring the ball is hitting the surface in the right spot.

"You can tell on the way down which part of the ball it's going to hit," he said. "I guess it probably depends if it is wet or dry. In dry weather it's pretty basic. You're trying to hit it on the front end of the ball so it bounces back to you."

Sometimes players can take too many bounces and upset the timing of their forwards' leads. Ablett is cognisant of that as he streams towards goal.

"It depends on the scenario," he said. "If I have a bit of space in front of me, then I definitely take a couple of extra bounces. It's very much a running game and bouncing the ball is a big part of today's game. We are encouraged when we are out in space and there is not a target up the field to run along and have a bounce."

Playing on good surfaces at Skilled Stadium, the MCG and Telstra Dome

RUN AND CARRY
Bouncing the ball has become a more valued skill with the modern "run and carry" approach to break open defences. Players fit the bounce neatly within their running stride while looking for their best disposal option.

each week makes it easier to bounce the ball with confidence.

"It helps playing on flat surfaces," Ablett said. "I remember playing local footy and we played on grounds that were very uneven, and that makes it hard."

Coaches instruct young players to practise kicking and handballing on their non-preferred side and Ablett says it is just as important to learn how to bounce the ball with either hand.

"If you're needing to take a bounce before you baulk around someone, and they're on your left-hand side, I think it's important that you bounce on your right (hand), and vice versa," he said.

"A lot of kids don't practise on their opposite sides, whether it's kicking, handballing or bouncing, because maybe they're a bit embarrassed around the rest of the group about stuffing up. But it will help your footy, whether it's at practice or in your spare time, to use both sides of your body."

Other great exponents of the running bounce in the AFL include Carlton's Chris Judd, North Melbourne's Brent Harvey, Melbourne's Aaron Davey and Western Bulldog pair Jason Akermanis and Ryan Griffen.

1 AT FULL STRIDE
Ablett, running at full stride, has started to bounce the ball with one hand slightly on top and pushing it down.

2 THE BOUNCE
His arm is fully extended as the ball is pushed down and bounced far enough in front so that it rebounds into his hands without him altering stride. The distance the ball is pushed in front depends on his speed – the faster he runs, the further in front.

3 WATCHING CLOSELY
The ball hits the ground on its front end at about 45 degrees and rotates forward as it rebounds towards his hands. He watches the ball closely throughout the bounce.

4 THE REBOUND
He watches the ball all the way back into his hands and takes it cleanly in both hands at mid-torso height.

5 ASSESSING OPTIONS
With the ball in both hands, Ablett continues to run downfield while looking for his next option. He must bounce the ball every 15 metres while running with it.

04
Tactical skills

//// Four-time premiership coach Allan Jeans defined tactics as "the methods deployed to exploit the weaknesses and negate the strengths of the opposition".

By their nature, tactics are intriguing sub-plots to the drama of a game of football. Simply identifying an opponent's relative strengths and weaknesses is one thing – and a daunting task at that – but then to devise ploys to expose and nullify them is infinitely tougher. Like many coaches before and since, Jeans' old sparring partner Ron Barassi loved all the secretive scheming and plotting for what he said was, from a coaching perspective, "a game of human chess".

Tactics are perhaps never more intriguing than when both teams have time to enact set-plays from situations such as stoppages (ball-ups and boundary throw-ins) and kick-ins. The team that wins the stoppages often wins the match and, as a result, clubs invest an enormous amount of time and effort in formulating ways to make clean getaways from these typically congested areas. They try to strike a balance between attack and defence, and players are often assigned specific roles at stoppages, including ball-winner, negator and sweeper, and often swap roles to make themselves less predictable to the opposition.

Kick-ins have been the subject of increasing consideration and planning since probably the mid-1980s when then Fitzroy coach Robert Walls introduced 'the huddle', in which his players, followed by their direct opponents, bunched up around centre half-back and, on a signal, made leads to space in all directions, or applied blocks to release one or two teammates. They got away with it for a season or two until then Collingwood coach Leigh Matthews instructed 'outriders' to guard the space their opponents wanted to run into.

These days most clubs employ intricate zone defences of up to 18 players, so the aim of a kick-in is to break the zone and, ideally, start a chain of passes that results in a scoring opportunity at the other end of the field. But with the designated kicker given just seven seconds before the field umpire calls "play on", the pressure is on to choose the right option and properly execute the kick because a mistake can cost a goal. Two superb designated kickers are the Western Bulldogs' Lindsay Gilbee and Collingwood's Heath Shaw.

There are numerous other examples of tactics relating to switching play to catch the opposition napping and open up the field of play for a coast-to-coast scoring chance, body positioning (explained by Fremantle captain Matthew Pavlich), the general requirement for midfielders and small forwards to be 'front and square' at packs (as demonstrated by the Bulldogs' Daniel Cross) and decision making (explained by Hawthorn premiership skipper Sam Mitchell).

Then there are the tactical adjustments required for different weather conditions. In the wet, players are instructed to get their bodies in line with the ball and flatten their hands at point of impact. In this section, we are enlightened by St Kilda legend Robert Harvey, who played in more varied conditions than perhaps any other player in the game's history.

QUICK THINKING:
Sam Mitchell grabs the ball against North Melbourne but he has a split second to decide how to dispose of it.

Decision making

//// Some players have the rare ability to appear to play the game as if they are in slow motion. This can be attributed for the most part to a sharpness of mind.

Sam Mitchell has been compared with dual Brownlow medallist Greg Williams and with good reason. Like Williams, Mitchell is not overly endowed with speed, but always seems to have time and space to execute his skills effectively.

"The players who aren't quite as fast sometimes need to get out of trouble a bit more than the others who are quicker," the Hawthorn premiership captain said. "As the game gets quicker, you get less time to make your decisions. You have to make sound decisions more quickly."

Mitchell is in that rare breed of players who make the game appear to be moving in slow-motion when the ball is in his vicinity – which can be attributed to his quick thinking on the field.

"Certain players seem to have that skill," he said. "Robert Harvey was a good example. He never looked like he was in too much of a rush.

"But if you do look like you're in a rush, that's not necessarily such a bad thing. Brent 'Boomer' Harvey and Chris Judd are very good decision makers because everything they do is very, very fast."

Mitchell said having strong structures within a team and good team rules makes decision making easier.

"The team plan makes you understand where your teammates are more likely to be," he said.

"Your teammates are going to be predictable to you and you're going to be predictable to them. When you pick up the ball, they are hopefully going to run to the place where you're going to give it to them."

Mitchell said his decision making has improved as he became more confident in his ability.

"If you're not confident, you might hesitate and second-guess yourself and that might take that half a second you didn't have and force you to make an error," he said. "If you have good confidence in the decision you make, it helps your disposal."

Mitchell believes peripheral vision and reflexes are important components of the decision-making process. But the process starts well before he gets the ball.

"I think that's one of the mistakes that quite often people make," he said. "For example, if you get the ball from a stoppage, you should have a reasonably good idea of where each player is on the ground so that you know what you're going to see when you take possession. You're just picking up smaller movements rather than taking it all in for the first time.

"The more you play with individual players, the better your decision making becomes. I've played a lot of footy with Robbie Campbell and we've played so much footy together for so long that every time he gets it or I get it, we know where each other is going to be. Then you can make quicker decisions and quicker decisions are usually better ones."

Mitchell said it was important to practise your decision making at training by performing drills under game-day pressure.

"You don't need to be too complicated," he said. "If you're at training and doing a drill involving decision making, don't take an extra couple of seconds just because you can because there is no pressure on you."

Body positioning

//// Matthew Pavlich excels at playing in front and protecting his position by blocking his opponent. Players need to develop strength in their legs and hips to hold their position.

Fremantle captain Matthew Pavlich is blessed with uncanny anticipation that allows him to know where the ball is going to land, enabling him to out-position his opponent in many contests.

Pavlich has played all over the ground – in the midfield, defence and up forward – but the fundamentals of body positioning remain constant. Players must protect the 'drop zone', where the ball is likely to fall, and ensure that they have contact with their opponent to enable them to push off and take possession when the ball arrives.

But there are differences that need to be taken into account when playing in various parts of the ground.

"In a ruck hit-out or scrimmage situation, the ball comes in from a close range, as distinct from judging the ball in flight from a kick from a longer distance into the forward line," Pavlich said.

"It is in the forefront of your mind that your body is in the right position, so you are able to push off or get to the contest before your opposition player. You need to have total comprehension about where your opponent is and where the ball is going to land, whether that be in a marking contest or in a stoppage situation."

Pavlich said players could improve their body-positioning skills with constant practice.

"There is no doubt you can teach and learn it, with many hours at training spent one on one just watching the ball flight and seeing what happens off the boot," he said. "Towards the end of each session, particularly during the season, we would do some level of one-on-one body work, whether it was around the midfield stoppages or a genuine one-on-one contest, to judge the ball flight, push off and get to that drop zone."

Pavlich said the 2005 change of the interpretation of the marking interference rule, which resulted in defenders being penalised for chopping the arms of their opponents in contests, has helped him as a forward.

"Now you're able to get your body into the right position and therefore have your arms outstretched," the Dockers star said. "If they do chop your arms, you're able to gain the free kick.

"The other one is the hands-in-the-back rule. Nowadays some defenders are playing in front because of that rule. It is getting harder and players have to adjust.

"Body positioning in that case is slightly different. It has become an art to be able to play in front, hold your ground and push back against the opposition player, knowing that they can't have their hands in the back."

For a player of his size (192cm, 101kg), Pavlich has excellent leg speed and admits that helps him take up the front position to win the ball over many opponents.

Pavlich said his father Steve, who played with West Torrens in the SANFL, had the biggest influence on him as a youngster on where to position his body, but he has played against some of the best exponents during his career, including Geelong full-back Matthew Scarlett, Adelaide defender Nathan Bock, Richmond forward Matthew Richardson and Essendon spearhead Matthew Lloyd.

"Watching AFL games now, you do pick traits that other players use," Pavlich said. "I've played on Richardson and Lloyd when I was playing in defence for a while. As a forward, there is no question Scarlett and Bock have become very good at it and there is no question Lloyd and Richardson have done it for a long time as key forwards."

Others who position their body well are dynamic Hawthorn forward Lance 'Buddy' Franklin, Brisbane Lions spearhead Daniel Bradshaw and Sydney forward Barry Hall.

TEACHING POINTS

1 Good body position can often be traced back to a player's ability to have a good 'starting position'. If a player is capable of taking front position in anticipation of the ball arriving, then he is a greater chance of having good body position.

2 As the ball is on its way to a contest, it is critical the attacking player protects the space where he believes the ball will land. He can protect this by using his body to block his opponent.

3 When the ball is just about to reach the area where it will land, the attacking player needs to push off his opponent and move towards the ball. The later the movement towards the ball, the less chance the defender will have to spoil.

USING HIS STRENGTH:
Matthew Pavlich is always trying to put his body in the right position so he can push off his opponent. Here he contests with Port Adelaide's Alipate Carlile, with both players watching the ball closely.

Front and square

//// **It is not only on the forward line where the ability to be front and square becomes important. By being in the right spot, and having the ability to read the ball off the pack, you can put your side to advantage.**

If you watch Western Bulldogs midfielder Daniel Cross in a game, it is easy to see why he picks up plenty of possessions.

Cross reads the game well and makes sure he is always in the best position to win the ball at either end of the ground.

In this sequence of photographs against Adelaide in 2008, Cross is front and square in the Bulldogs' defensive zone, ready to take the ball off the pack should it fall his way.

"As a wingman, my role is to get back and help out the defenders," Cross said. "Standing in that position, you want to watch the flight of the ball coming in, especially when you know your defender has got his forward covered.

"You want to get your feet well planted and, watching the ball come off the pack, you have to be on your toes as well.

"It's a very dynamic game and the ball can fly anywhere. You need to be adaptable in which way the ball will go."

2 **READING THE BALL**
In that balanced position, on his toes, he is watching the ball closely, as well as the contesting players' hands, to try and read which way the ball will spill.

3 **POSSESSION**
As he sees the ball come off the pack, he is immediately moving to gain possession of it.

Cross said being balanced and having good reflexes were important when he was in the front-and-square position.

"To be in that position, your reflexes are as important as anything," he said. "That's something that I practise every day during the season, especially with our specialist coaches. Having quick hands, that's one of my strengths that I have to use to be at the top of my game."

Cross said it was important to have a good understanding with teammates. "If there is already someone up the back, you don't need to run to the back of the pack, or vice-versa," he said.

On the forward line, players who are front and square are often moving quickly as they go for goal. "In defence you want to be more stable and be assured you're going to get the ball to clear it from that zone," the Bulldogs midfielder said.

"Going forward, you might read the ball into the pack the same way, but you might hit it with a bit more speed to try to burst through the pack and maybe snap a goal."

Cross said one of the best exponents in the AFL of being front and square was livewire Collingwood forward Leon Davis. North Melbourne's Matt Campbell, St Kilda's Stephen Milne and Carlton's Eddie Betts were also proficient at this skill.

"Jarrod Harbrow is our young crumbing forward with a lot of speed," Cross said.

TEACHING POINTS

1 Whenever players contest a ball in the air, the large majority of the time the ball will fall forward of the contest, hence the need to be front and square.

2 It is important when front and square to be balanced and fairly stationary. A player moving at speed will find it more difficult to time his run to the fall of the ball.

3 The direction the players' hands (palms) are facing is often a good clue as to which way the ball will fall.

Adverse weather

//// **Robert Harvey saw it all in his illustrious career. A true measure of his greatness was his ability to adapt to any conditions that he had to encounter, be it rain and hail in Melbourne and Adelaide or sunshine in Brisbane and Perth.**

In 21 seasons former St Kilda champion Robert Harvey encountered many and varied conditions over 383 memorable matches.

Growing up in Melbourne, Harvey found it easier to adapt to cold, wet conditions than to extreme heat, particularly in places such as Brisbane or Perth.

But he said the introduction of protective measures such as ice vests and fans, as well as increased use of interchange bench rotations, helped him cope later in his career.

"I remember a few early games in Perth and especially Brisbane, where it was probably more humid, that I was just really struggling in the early days," Harvey said. "I was struggled with cramp, so I did some stuff to try to negate that a bit when I was playing in hot weather."

Harvey had plenty of practice adjusting to difficult conditions, training regularly in the mud and slush at Moorabbin and Waverley Park. "I grew up with it, not that I liked it, particularly as a kid playing in cold,

HAIL THE HEROES: Port Adelaide and St Kilda players, including Robert Harvey (second from left), battle atrocious conditions at AAMI Stadium in 2007.

wet conditions," Harvey said. "That's what the game is about. It's a winter game, so we're used to that. You never miss a session because it's too wet."

Harvey said it was important to practise your skills in the wet to make the transition to adverse conditions easier. The major adjustments players need to make include flattening your hands at point of contact and ensuring your body is in line with the ball.

"Even kicking in the wet is different," he said. "The ball is heavier, so it doesn't go as far. You have to really weight your kicks, especially if you're kicking to a lead."

When he started his senior career with the Saints in 1988, playing on muddy surfaces at venues such as Moorabbin,

Waverley Park, Princes Park, Whitten Oval, Victoria Park and Windy Hill was common-place.

"Often the cricket pitches were left in the middle of the ground and the grass around the flanks tended to get boggy if it was wet," Harvey said.

"Now the grounds have better drainage, so we don't get those boggy patches. You can barely remember the last time the MCG was muddy, so you don't have to practise for wet-weather conditions that much now."

Harvey recalled the match pictured above, describing the conditions at AAMI Stadium in 2007 as among the worst he played in. "The pain of getting hit by the hailstones was huge," he said.

The worst conditions he encountered were in a Teal Cup match in Canberra, before he started his VFL/AFL career.

"Manuka Oval was a lake with the amount of water on the ground," he said.

But, while those conditions were challenging, his preference was to play in the wet rather than have to contend with strong winds.

"In the last 10 years of my career, I didn't play in many windy games because you're playing in good stadiums with high stands," said Harvey, who played the twilight of his career under the roof at Telstra Dome.

"It's definitely harder to play in the wind. The wind can be really frustrating and often the play is on one side of the ground."

Stoppages

//// Split-second decisions that can determine the outcome of a contest are made at every stoppage. Therefore, sides try to set up to cover all contingencies.

Winning stoppages is crucial. At each stoppage, teams are trying to execute a pre-arranged and well-drilled plan.

The ideal is for the ruckman to hit the ball to a teammate who is on the move either in the direction of goal or moving away from goal into space.

Some teams use a theoretical clock face to quickly communicate where they want the ball to be hit. Unless one ruckman is dominating, teams cover all bases at stoppages, employing a go-to person, a blocker and a sweeper at centre square stoppages (see definitions in box).

Teams must hedge their bets between defence and attack because a quick, clean clearance to the opposition will inevitably end in a scoring opportunity.

Former West Coast star and Collingwood assistant coach Guy McKenna, now overseeing the new Gold Coast team, was in charge of stoppages for the Dream Team during the Hall of Fame Tribute Match against Victoria at the MCG in May, 2008.

He concedes the decisions made at stoppages are sometimes football's equivalent of Russian roulette. "It's totally a judgment call," he said.

The best midfield combinations have a balance of ball hunters, man hunters and space hunters.

Good players can fulfil several roles, happy to pick up a man but then roll off them into space if their teammate wins the ball.

They can also tighten up if the opposition wins it.

As soon as the ball is bounced, each player at the stoppage has a split-second decision to make.

Does he try to win possession? Does he peel off into space? Does he play tight and stay on his man?

"That's how stoppage players live their life," McKenna said.

"If you can hold the ball up or slow the ball down, it doesn't matter where your opponent is, but if you make that call to affect the contest and get in there and lose the ball or lose position and the opposition get it, then your man is going to bite you on the backside by heading back or running forward to hurt you at that stoppage."

All sides are well-drilled when it comes to stoppages with some, such as recent premiership sides Hawthorn, Geelong and Sydney, leading the way with their tactics.

ROLES AT STOPPAGES

GO-TO PLAYER: Attacking player looking to receive the ball from the ruckman or quickly adopt a defensive role if the ball goes the opposition's way.

SWEEPER: Like a goalkeeper, the sweeper is the last line of defence if an opponent receives the ball. Has to force the opposition to at least kick the ball under pressure so the backline can have an impact on the next contest.

BLOCKER: Either protects the space for the go-to player to receive the ball or blocks opponents from moving into the hit zone.

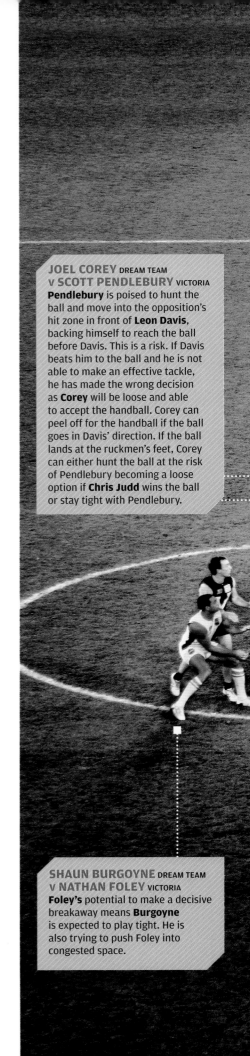

JOEL COREY DREAM TEAM **v SCOTT PENDLEBURY** VICTORIA
Pendlebury is poised to hunt the ball and move into the opposition's hit zone in front of **Leon Davis**, backing himself to reach the ball before Davis. This is a risk. If Davis beats him to the ball and he is not able to make an effective tackle, he has made the wrong decision as **Corey** will be loose and able to accept the handball. Corey can peel off for the handball if the ball goes in Davis' direction. If the ball lands at the ruckmen's feet, Corey can either hunt the ball at the risk of Pendlebury becoming a loose option if **Chris Judd** wins the ball or stay tight with Pendlebury.

SHAUN BURGOYNE DREAM TEAM **v NATHAN FOLEY** VICTORIA
Foley's potential to make a decisive breakaway means **Burgoyne** is expected to play tight. He is also trying to push Foley into congested space.

AUSTRALIAN FOOTBALL 150 YEARS

DEAN COX DREAM TEAM **v JOSH FRASER** VICTORIA
Cox attempts to palm the ball into the space in front of **Leon Davis**, the likely go-to man. **Fraser** is looking to push the ball away from that space for **Chris Judd**, **Nathan Foley** or **Sam Mitchell** to run on to. Cox looks to have the ascendancy.

BRETT KIRK DREAM TEAM **v SAM MITCHELL** VICTORIA
Put the best negating player in the game on the best winner of the ball at stoppages. **Kirk** is also blocking **Mitchell** from moving into the space **Dean Cox** is attempting to hit the ball into, keeping the hit zone free of opponents.

LEON DAVIS DREAM TEAM **v LUKE POWER** VICTORIA
Davis moved from the forward line to become the go-to player. He has space in front of him and **Dean Cox** is aiming to tap the ball in his direction. **Power** should be tighter, but has an advantage if Victoria wins the ball.

KANE CORNES DREAM TEAM **v CHRIS JUDD** VICTORIA
In his defensive role, **Cornes** is trying to edge **Judd** into **Joel Corey** and the ruckman, denying Judd space to run into and staying close while the ball is in dispute. Judd is looking to win the ball.

SIMON GOODWIN DREAM TEAM **v RYAN O'KEEFE** VICTORIA
Goodwin backs **Dean Cox** to win the tap to **Leon Davis**. If Davis beats **Scott Pendlebury** to the ball and handballs to **Joel Corey** in space, then Goodwin can be a spare option forward. **O'Keefe** will roll the dice if the ball is in dispute, either pushing forward himself or playing tight on Goodwin. O'Keefe is also a slim chance to receive **Josh Fraser's** tap.

COREY ENRIGHT DREAM TEAM **v ADAM GOODES** VICTORIA
Enright touches **Goodes** and stays between the ball and his opponent to ensure Goodes can't run past for the handball.

4
Tyson Goldsack

1
Heath Shaw

The kick-in

//// AFL clubs put vast amounts of time, energy and science into effectively bringing the ball back into play after a behind. It is considered so important because, in a close contest, this can be the difference between winning and losing.

Twelve seconds. You stand alone in the defensive goalsquare, the Sherrin spinning nervously in your hands. Ten. The opposition, desperate to retain the ball in attack, quickly forms its kick-in zone. Eight. Teammates fan out in all directions, some gesturing frantically, others screaming for the ball. Six. The opposition cheer squad thumps on the fence behind you, hurling abuse. Four. The man on the mark crouches hungrily, daring you to play on. Two.

Decision time – what you do next could change the course of the match. One. "Play on, play on!" yells the field umpire.

Welcome to the high-pressure world of kick-ins, where a false move will probably cost a goal, or a well-executed play could set up an attacking thrust. As the game becomes more tactically structured, the importance of the kick-in has grown accordingly.

Collingwood defensive coach Mark Neeld feels, first and foremost, a kick-in taker must be a sound, yet speedy decision maker.

2 Dane Swan

Adelaide runner **3**

6 Marty Clarke

8 Ben Johnson

5 Nathan Brown

Chris Bryan **7**

BREAKING THE ZONE

Magpie **Heath Shaw** (1) is confronted with a 15-man Adelaide zone at a kick-in (some players not shown). However, due to the tag placed on **Dane Swan** (2), a gap has opened up in the right half-back area near the Adelaide runner (3). **Tyson Goldsack** (4), **Nathan Brown** (5), **Marty Clarke** (6) and **Chris Bryan** (7) run away from this space so as not to clutter the area, while Shaw signals teammate **Ben Johnson** (8) to offer a lead.

"You need to decide straight away whether you can take on the guy on the mark and beat him," Neeld said. "Most clubs will instruct the player who has the ball to do a 'fast play' if he can, especially nowadays not having to wait for the goal umpire to wave his flag."

If playing on or moving the ball fluently is not possible, the designated kicker needs to identify the opposition's tactics quickly. Typically, a team will employ a 12, 15 or (as utilised by Hawthorn in recent times) 18-man zone.

"A lot of teams will go quickly into a 12-man formation, but if the player kicking in takes too long, 18 players can get the chance to set up," Neeld said.

Recognition of opposition structure assists with picking out potential gaps and weaknesses. For example, the 18-man zone can be exposed with quick ball movement through the middle, catching opposition defenders out of position.

And while foot skills are clearly a must for kick-ins, those with different kicking strengths can be utilised to counteract various zones.

"Teams will have designated kickers for different types of set plays," Neeld said. "At Collingwood, we'll do whole ground activities with two sides and practise kicking against a variety of zones. If we want a short kick to pinpoint through the zone, we'll use a particular player.

If we've decided that the other side is susceptible at the back of the zone, we'll use a bloke who can kick the ball long and flat. Or if there's a team with short wingmen, we'll use someone who can put the ball up long and high to allow a tall centre half-back or ruckman to come over the top."

Last but not least, an effective taker of the kick-in needs to have the courage of his convictions.

"It's not the traditional courage of running back with the flight of the ball against Jonathan Brown, but it's still courage," Neeld said. "You have to have that steely nerve to hit a player with only five metres of space each side."

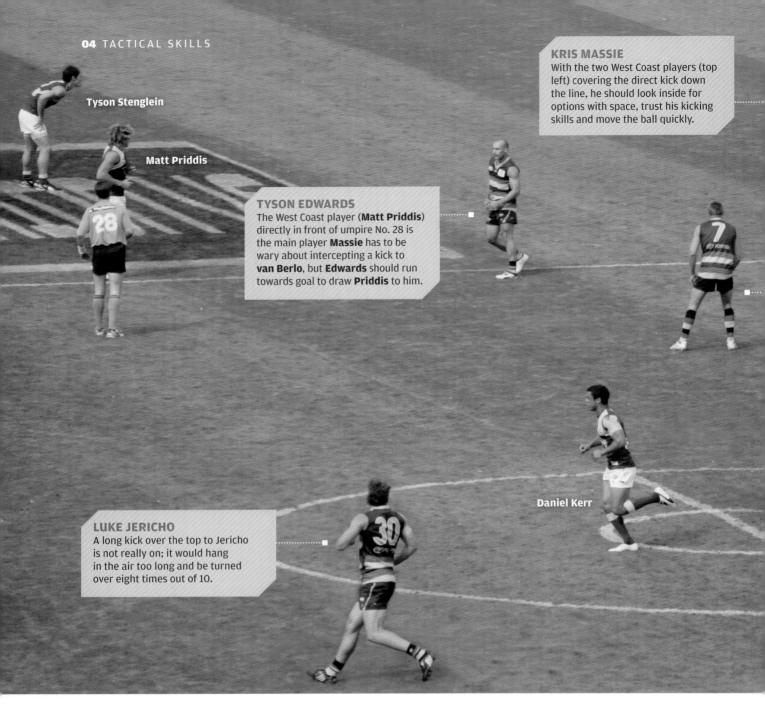

Tyson Stenglein

Matt Priddis

KRIS MASSIE
With the two West Coast players (top left) covering the direct kick down the line, he should look inside for options with space, trust his kicking skills and move the ball quickly.

TYSON EDWARDS
The West Coast player (**Matt Priddis**) directly in front of umpire No. 28 is the main player **Massie** has to be wary about intercepting a kick to **van Berlo**, but **Edwards** should run towards goal to draw **Priddis** to him.

Daniel Kerr

LUKE JERICHO
A long kick over the top to Jericho is not really on; it would hang in the air too long and be turned over eight times out of 10.

Switching play

//// In a distinguished career with Adelaide, Ben Hart was a fine exponent of switching the play. Now an assistant coach with the Crows, Hart explains how, when used properly, the tactic remains one of the best ways to bypass defensive zones.

Kicking across your opponent's goal-face was once regarded as a football sin, but switching play, both in defence and further up the ground, is an essential tactic used by every AFL side today.

Adelaide assistant coach Ben Hart says teams rely on switches of play to penetrate the zones routinely used all over the ground in the modern game.

"(Switching play) has got to be in your playbook these days if you want to be able

to go through or around a zone," Hart said.

"It's something generally used when there are opposition numbers in front of you down the line and it's one way of opening the play and moving the ball into space."

While a player needed good vision and decision-making skills to switch play successfully, Hart stressed without accurate kicking and quick ball movement, any such attempts were likely to come unstuck.

"Having the skills to be able to hit your target with your kick is obviously very

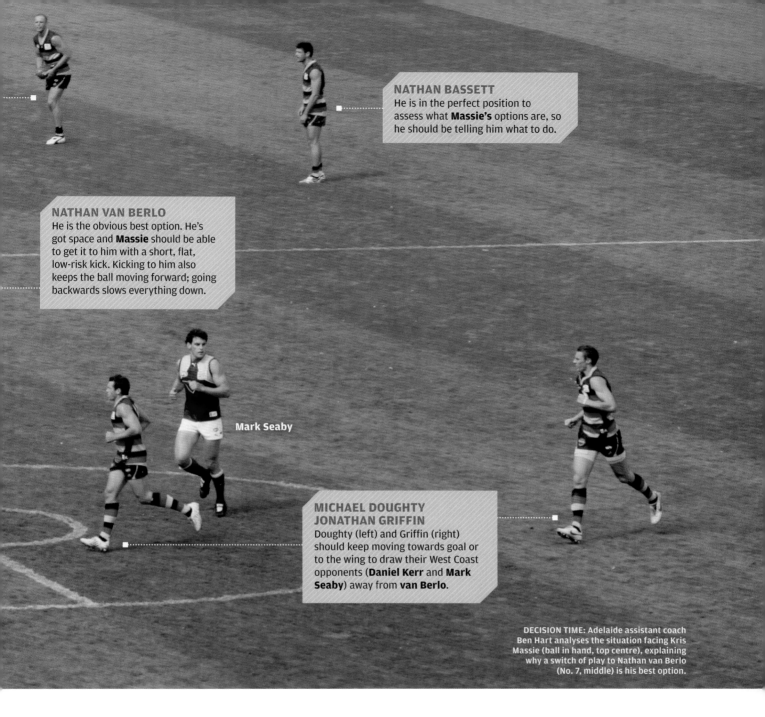

NATHAN BASSETT
He is in the perfect position to assess what **Massie's** options are, so he should be telling him what to do.

NATHAN VAN BERLO
He is the obvious best option. He's got space and **Massie** should be able to get it to him with a short, flat, low-risk kick. Kicking to him also keeps the ball moving forward; going backwards slows everything down.

Mark Seaby

MICHAEL DOUGHTY
JONATHAN GRIFFIN
Doughty (left) and Griffin (right) should keep moving towards goal or to the wing to draw their West Coast opponents (**Daniel Kerr** and **Mark Seaby**) away from **van Berlo**.

DECISION TIME: Adelaide assistant coach Ben Hart analyses the situation facing Kris Massie (ball in hand, top centre), explaining why a switch of play to Nathan van Berlo (No. 7, middle) is his best option.

important, but so, too, is your speed of ball movement – the quicker you move it, the less chance the opposition has of cutting it off," Hart said.

To achieve this, Hart said it was generally best to switch play with short kicks.

"The key is short, flat, accurate kicks," he said. "I think it's better to use two or three short kicks to move the ball out to the other side rather than going with one long kick, which will hang in the air a little bit longer and give the opposition more of a chance to cut it off."

For this reason, Hart, in referring to the picture above, said Kris Massie's best option was a short pass to Nathan van Berlo (No. 7), rather than a longer kick to Luke

Jericho (No. 30), despite the fact both players were in space.

He singled out Tyson Edwards and Nathan Bassett as players at the Crows whose strong kicking skills had made them particularly adept at switching the play, while nominating Hawthorn's Luke Hodge as one of the best from the other clubs.

"These guys have that ability to hit their targets with their kicks all the time," Hart said. "Not only that but they've also got the foot skills to be able to hit the type of flat kick you need to make a switch with very little risk – they give the opposition virtually no chance of effecting a turnover."

For a switch of play to penetrate opposition zones, Hart said kicking

backwards should be avoided. "One of the main things is you don't want to go too far backwards," he said. "As soon as you start going backwards, it slows everything down and gives the opposition time to adjust."

Hart said the player attempting to switch play was also reliant on his surrounding teammates' help. He needed to be able to assess quickly who his best option was and then draw opposition players away from that player by running down or across the ground.

In teaching players how to switch the play, Hart said coaches primarily relied on simulated situations in intra-club match play and on drills that emphasised kicking to the teammate in the best position.

OUT OF MY WAY: There is no better sight in football than Brisbane Lion Jared Brennan scooping the ball up one-handed and sprinting away.

05
Evasive skills

//// It takes great skill and athleticism to evade an opponent, particularly at top speed, but a well-executed side-step or blind turn is a sight to behold.

There is nothing like watching a magician at work, waving the ball around like a wand and mesmerising those unfortunates vainly attempting to tackle or even corral them.

Players who boast the sheer evasive skills and audacity to dodge and weave around their pursuers are among the game's most aesthetically pleasing features. Indeed, it's poetry in motion.

Past greats such as Collingwood genius Peter Daicos, Hawthorn and Adelaide champion Darren Jarman and Essendon superstar James Hird were lacking in leg speed but their loose hips, deft feet and razor-sharp wits made them virtually untouchable in their primes.

They were masters of manoeuvres such as the baulk, side-step and blind turn and knew how to maximise the limited speed they possessed.

Interestingly, our exponents of the side-step and blind turn – Western Bulldog midfielder Ryan Griffen and North Melbourne skipper Brent Harvey

respectively – are endowed with genuine pace, which adds another dimension to their considerable evasive abilities.

Also intriguing is that Griffen is an example of a relatively new breed of athlete – perhaps with Hawthorn superstar Lance Franklin heading the list – that breaks the mould when it comes to elusiveness because of his sheer size. Despite his 188cm and 88kg, Griffen is surprisingly agile and light on his feet.

Harvey is at the other end of the size spectrum, his 172cm/76kg frame often appearing to run into trouble before, in the blink of an eye, he pirouettes away from a tackle and is suddenly bounding in space through the Kangaroos midfield. Interesting to note that he based his technique on another Harvey, St Kilda legend Robert, whose trademark 'shimmy' or 'hippy-hippy shake' sent Saints fans into swooning hysterics.

Another heart-and-soul former Saint skipper, Lenny Hayes, is a superb exponent of the fend. The tough midfielder's great balance and core strength enable him to ward off

opponents by pushing them in the chest or brushing away their flailing arms as he powers through tackles without seeming to lose forward momentum.

Although evasive skills can and are practised regularly by players, some of the best exponents believe their showcasing of them are largely the result of instinctive, split-second decisions they don't even have to think about.

Players with proven ability to evade opponents are generally given a licence by their coaches to play their natural games and take on the opposition to create more run and scoring opportunities, even in the knowledge that occasionally they will be tackled and possibly penalised for holding the ball. The reward is often worth the calculated risk.

Running technique is also vital to a player's ability to evade, and to this end we have sought the advice of one of the fastest players in the AFL, Melbourne speedster Aaron Davey, to explain the important technical aspects of running.

1 **PREPARATION**
Harvey is approaching his opponent with the ball held in both hands while watching the opponent closely.

2 **PLANT**
He steps to the right and holds the ball out to the right in front of his opponent to draw him towards the ball.

Blind turn

//// The blind turn is a spectacular way for nimble, smart players to create space and launch attacks from any part of the ground. If the skill is executed well, it can lift a side and leave the opposition floundering in its wake.

North Melbourne captain Brent Harvey makes it look easy when he performs a trademark blind turn around a hapless opponent.

It is a skill that has been years in the making for the Kangaroos star, but it is something that comes naturally to him.

"I don't really practise it. It's really an instinctive thing," Harvey said.

"When you muck around with the boys, you probably practise it more than actually

in training. You can't plan it because if you plan it you always get tackled."

Harvey said his role model for one of his signature moves was retired St Kilda champion Robert Harvey.

"He's easily the best I've seen at it," the Roos veteran said. "You can see the way he does it, he doesn't think about the way he's going to do it. If someone overcommits, he's gone with either a baulk or a blind turn."

Harvey said making a blind turn required a split-second decision. "I think once the

3 DRIVE
Harvey begins to turn to the right in front of his opponent, swinging away from him, yet at the same time bringing the ball in close to his body in the hand furthest away from danger. This turning motion makes it difficult to tackle him.

4 TIGHT TURN
He continues to turn in towards the centre of the ground, keeping his body low and compact to facilitate the tight turn and holding the ball tightly to his body.

5 ACCELERATION
As he comes out of the turn, Harvey begins to accelerate away before straightening up his body and looking for the next attacking option.

opposition is committed and they look like they're going to smother the ball, you can pull out and get around them," he said. "Hopefully you can take up some more ground and get the ball forward."

Haarvey is always aware of who is around him before attempting a blind turn.

"You know the bloke who's usually chasing you," he said. "I'd normally have a look to see what sort of player it is because if it's a player with the pace of (teammates) Matt Campbell or Daniel Wells, I'm not too keen on taking those sort of guys on. If you get one of the big ruckmen who takes the big steps, you can get around them fairly easily."

Harvey is given plenty of freedom by coach Dean Laidley, who is happy for him to perform the skill on any part of the ground.

"There's a few of us who have got a bit of a licence and fortunately I'm one of them," the midfielder said. "If you get caught, so be it. Every now and then you're going to get tackled.

"When you're running the ball out of the backline, it's a good opportunity to do it. It's certainly OK to do it through the midfield. If you can get around someone and have a shot at goal, you always take those chances."

Harvey said it was easier for smaller, quicker players such as himself to perform the skill rather than a ruckman or centre half-forward.

TEACHING POINTS

The blind turn is most commonly used to evade an opponent when a player is being chased from behind.

1 As the opponent gets closer, hold the ball out to one side.

2 Dig the foot on that side in to the ground to push hard to the opposite side.

3 Pull the ball back in quickly to a secure position as you turn your body away from your opponent.

4 Accelerate away quickly.

1 PREPARATION
Griffen is watching his opponent closely and shuffling in preparation for stepping around the player. He is moving the ball out towards the left side to draw his opponent towards the ball.

2 PLANT
He plants his left foot and is beginning to transfer the ball to the right side away from his opponent, and preparing to push hard to the right.

Side-step

//// Western Bulldogs star Ryan Griffen loves to get around opponents and leave them standing as he charges downfield to launch another attack. It is a skill that has been perfected by many players and can be practised easily.

Western Bulldogs fans have seen Ryan Griffen use the side-step with great effect since he made his AFL debut in 2005.

The solid midfielder often leaves opponents standing as he darts around them with deft use of the feet.

Before he is about to use the side-step, Griffen shuffles his feet and waits for an opponent to make their move. "Then I'll push off the other way to try to trick them," he said. "It's not easy to do, but when it does work, it looks all right."

The decision when and where to use the side-step is instinctive. It creates time and space for Griffen in tight situations. "It's a split-second decision. If a player comes at me quickly in a pack, I'll use it then and try to get around them," he said.

"When I'm running down the wing taking a bounce, I try not to use it. I try to dispose of the ball before they tackle me because I've got time."

3 DRIVE
Griffen drives hard off his planted left foot, away from the player attempting to tackle, with the ball in a safe position on the right side of his body. He is looking up the field for his next attacking option.

4 ACCELERATION
He accelerates away from the tackler, scanning for the best option. He is carrying the ball in two hands to allow efficient preparation for delivery by either hand or foot on both sides.

Griffen has used the side-step since he started as a junior.

While he has become an expert at this skill over time, he continues to work on it at training.

"I use it every time I go out on the training track because that's just the way I play," he said. "We do tackling training, where you have to try to get around your opponent, and I use the side-step then."

Griffen has improved in his ability to execute the skill.

"I guess it has improved because you do leg weights and you become a lot stronger through the legs," he said.

Griffen grew up in Adelaide and marvelled at the ease with which Crows veteran Andrew McLeod could avoid trouble with the side-step.

Among the better exponents of the side-step are Port Adelaide rover David Rodan and North Melbourne captain Brent Harvey, two of the best small men in the AFL. Interestingly, both are 'low-to-the-ground' players and keep their feet and balance superbly.

Griffen's coach Rodney Eade encourages him to use the side-step, which gives him extra confidence.

"He has just told me to use my natural talent and that's what I try to do," Griffen said. "I've been caught before and 'Rocket' has never come down on me."

TEACHING POINTS

1 Hold the ball out to one side as the opponent approaches.

2 Push hard off the planted foot.

3 Pull the ball back in quickly to a secure position as you step around your opponent.

4 Ensure that you change direction during the step.

NOTE: As you will be deemed to have had prior opportunity if you take on an opponent, it is important that if you are tackled, you keep your arms free so that you can immediately (and effectively) dispose of the ball.

1 PREPARATION
Hayes keeps a close eye on his opponent as he comes towards him and is well balanced to fend him off.

2 ARM EXTENSION
He braces himself for contact and extends the left arm while protecting the ball with his right arm. His fending-off arm is rigid, but has a slight bend in it to allow for impact and controlled force to be applied.

Fending off

//// **This is common in other football codes and has proved useful for AFL players as well. St Kilda midfielder Lenny Hayes employs the fend to create space and evade the clutches of opponents preparing to tackle.**

Using a legitimate fend to ward off opponents is a natural instinct for St Kilda star Lenny Hayes.

Growing up in Sydney, Hayes played rugby league and rugby union in his junior days before switching to Australian Football. As a youngster, he would practise the fend in the backyard with his brother.

Hayes uses the fend at a stoppage to create space or evade an oncoming tackler when he is on the run, regardless of the size of his opponent.

"If someone is gaining ground on you and makes a dive to tackle you, it helps if you can get an arm out," he said. "You'd like to get the ball off, but it happens pretty quickly, so sometimes you have to push off an opponent. It's just a reaction where you stick the arm out to get away.

"I'm not the quickest guy around, so sometimes you have to use the fend to try to get away."

3 FEND-OFF

Hayes keeps his eyes on his opponent as he is careful to ensure his fending-off arm makes contact with his opponent's chest and he avoids high contact. Hayes' aim is to halt the opponent's momentum towards him.

4 ACCELERATION

Once impact has been made between Hayes' hand and the opponent's chest, the Saint will push off his opponent and accelerate away.

It is important not to infringe when applying the fend.

"You can't get the guys too high," Hayes said. "You aim for the chest."

St Kilda players are encouraged to use the fend at training during tackling practice, but Hayes does not use the fend as much as he used to in matches because the tackling skills throughout the AFL have improved.

"It's probably a lot harder today because we do a lot of tackling practice and guys are told to knock that arm away if someone is fending you," he said. "Players also try to get underneath the arm used to fend off."

Some of the best exponents in the AFL include Hawthorn's Lance 'Buddy'

Franklin and Luke Hodge, Geelong's Gary Ablett, Carlton's Chris Judd and North Melbourne's Daniel Harris.

When one of Franklin's long arms is outstretched, it is difficult for an opponent to lay a hand on him and he is hard to stop in full flight.

"He's probably the best out there," Hayes said. "You see Buddy doing it every second week. Brad Sewell is hard to tackle as well. He uses his strength and the fend-off really well."

Hayes said players with a rugby league or union background such as his teammate Sam Gilbert and Essendon midfielder Mark McVeigh were also excellent exponents.

TEACHING POINTS

1 It is important when fending not to jump off the ground and to be in a balanced position.

2 The fending-off arm needs to be strong and slightly flexed, allowing force to be applied.

3 Once contact has been made, a player should push off the tackler.

NOTE: As you will be deemed to have had prior opportunity if you take on an opponent, it is important that if you are tackled, you keep your arms free so that you can immediately (and effectively) dispose of the ball.

RUNNING SMART:
Aaron Davey is now timing his run so he can be more damaging throughout games, as he leads Western Bulldogs midfielder Adam Cooney to the ball.

Running technique

//// Even the AFL's fastest players can become quicker with improved running technique. But in today's non-stop game, they must learn when and where to use their pace.

Melbourne's Aaron Davey has been blessed with amazing speed, yet he continues to work on becoming even quicker.

Davey has been terrifying backmen since he burst on to the AFL scene in 2004. His trademark soon became his run-down tackle, where he would concede an opponent a healthy head start before putting on the 'after-burners' to bring him down.

Davey said while his speed had always been his greatest asset as a player, when he started working with Melbourne athletic development coach Bohdan Babijczuk two years ago he soon discovered his running technique had room for improvement.

Specifically, Babijczuk identified that Davey was not using his arms enough when he ran, losing speed by not driving them back far enough. And when taking off from a standing start Davey was coming up into an upright position too quickly and then was not lifting his knees high enough.

"To run at your fastest you need the arms and legs to be working together, but not using my arms enough affected that arm-leg coordination," Davey said.

"And with your take-off you've got to push and drive for the first 10 or 20m and to do that you've got to stay down rather than coming up straight away."

Davey said he was still working hard on improving these aspects of his running technique through regular sessions with Babijczuk, as well as running drills that encouraged quick, short steps and a high knee lift.

While injuries set him back in 2007 and 2008, Davey could feel his hard work already paying off.

"I have noticed a change in my pace and when I take off I just feel a bit lighter and stronger in my legs," he said.

An AFL player's training involves a mix of sprinting and endurance work, but Davey says technique is not so important with distance running.

"With the longer stuff it's based around trying to get people to develop a good (fitness) base, where you can run at a good but really controlled pace," he said.

"It's mainly about getting in a rhythm where you're nice and relaxed and not trying too hard."

But just as important, Davey said, was learning the art of "running smart" during a game.

"I can get caught up in trying to go the fastest I can every time I go for the ball," he said. "But sometimes I'd be better off maybe going at 80 per cent and being smart about where I'm running so I can run out games better. I'm still trying to find that balance."

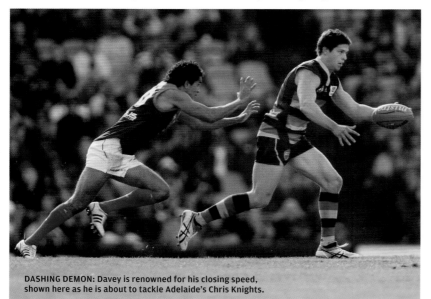

DASHING DEMON: Davey is renowned for his closing speed, shown here as he is about to tackle Adelaide's Chris Knights.

HOW TO LIFT THE PACE

1. Moving arms and legs in a straight line and not across the body.
2. Arms and legs working in unison – high knee lift, arms pumping.
3. Keeping head and trunk steady – eyes looking ahead.

STOPPED IN HIS TRACKS:
Hawthorn youngster
Cyril Rioli executes the
ideal smother on North
Melbourne's Daniel Harris.

06
One-percenters

//// Courageous acts on the football field can inspire teams to great heights, be it a perfect smother, a team-lifting shepherd, a timely spoil or a legal bump.

They don't rate a mention in any newspaper stats column and aren't at the forefront of your mind when fans think about the features that make Australian Football such a great spectacle, but they are highly valued by coaches, teammates and appreciative fans.

They are acts of sheer desperation – spoils, shepherds, smothers and bumps – known as 'one-percenters' because there are numerous opportunities for players to apply them in a match.

When one-percenters are executed properly, coaches highlight them to players as shining examples of self-sacrifice, hardness and team play.

The beauty of one-percenters is anyone can perform them. It's not about talent; it's about attitude. Players just need to be disciplined, 'switched on' and committed to the team cause. And talented footballers who master them become more valuable, complete and respected by their peers.

There are few more appreciated one-percenters than the shepherd, especially in modern football where numerous players flood stoppages and make it difficult for clean clearances.

A fine exponent of the shepherd is Carlton utility Jarrad Waite, who protects and releases Blues teammates by using his long limbs to block would-be tacklers.

Applying an effective shepherd can mean the difference between a teammate being tackled, making an error through hurried disposal or breaking clear to create play.

Spoiling is another one-percenter that relies on a timely, disciplined action. There is little worse for a coach than seeing one of his players get out-marked when he should have punched from behind – it's one of the oldest and most basic fundamentals of the game, particularly for defenders.

But while some players would risk a low-percentage marking attempt from behind, a disciplined team man such as Adelaide utility Graham Johncock will usually fist the ball clear of the danger area. It can also be an attacking move because often the ball is knocked 10-20 metres from the pack and can alter the momentum of a passage of play, and perhaps even the course of a match.

The same applies to a smother: just when a player appears certain to launch the ball forward, a smother can immediately have the ball moving in the opposite direction. North Melbourne veteran Adam Simpson has never shied away from the potentially finger-jarring sensation. It takes guts to smother with your hands, especially on a cold day.

An old-fashioned highlight of our game is the bump, as is often applied by Fremantle tagger Ryan Crowley.

Among the memorable bumps of the past were those dished out by Richmond's Laurie Fowler on Carlton captain-coach John Nicholls in the 1973 Grand Final, and Hawthorn's Dermott Brereton on Essendon's Paul Vander Haar in the 1989 second semi-final. Although rule changes have made the head sacrosanct, there is still an element of perverse poetry in seeing a perfectly timed hip-and-shoulder.

Smother

//// Former North Melbourne captain Adam Simpson has pulled off a few spectacular smothers over the years and says they have the ability to lift a team.

Coaches often talk about the "one-percenters" that make a difference in a tight encounter. Fans love to see their heroes making a desperate lunge at an opponent and the perfect smother can lift a side. Former North Melbourne captain Adam Simpson remains one of the best exponents of this skill in the AFL.

"You don't have to have talent to be good at smothering, it's definitely a mindset," Simpson said. "Everyone has got the ability to do something like that. When you see your teammate doing it, it just shows that you're switched on and the team is willing to do anything to win the game.

"For me, it's the one when someone is on the run and you can do that big dive across the leg to smother the ball. The diving smothers to prevent a shot on goal are the ones you remember."

While the Kangaroos do not practise the smother much at training, Simpson and his teammates get in a few in the rooms as a warm-up before games.

"We get a bit of body contact and do a few practice tackles, then do a few practice smothers, so we're up and about for the game," Simpson said. "We get someone to kick the ball as hard as they can."

Simpson has played with some of the best exponents of the smother.

"Byron Pickett was probably one of the best. He was very good at anticipating when the ball was going to be kicked and timing it so the smother was pure," he said. "Anthony Stevens used to do a couple of rippers every year. Glenn Archer was good and I've seen Drew (Petrie) do them as well."

Simpson said he would try to make a smother when it was too late to tackle an opponent. "All you can do is prevent the disposal being effective and that's when you might try to smother," he said.

Other players who are noted for their ability to smother include Collingwood captain Nick Maxwell, Hawthorn skipper Sam Mitchell and Geelong midfielder Cameron Ling.

But the increased pace of the game and changes to the way AFL football is played has made it more difficult to smother the ball.

Simpson said smothering the ball was a courageous act, but rated other "one-percenters" such as dropping back into the hole as more courageous.

BODY ON THE LINE: Adam Simpson is about to receive the full brunt of a kick from young Sydney Swan Kieren Jack.

TEACHING POINTS

1 Get as close as possible to the player with the ball.

2 Hands are thrust straight out from the hip across the direction of the kick. They are not raised above the head and brought down on the foot.

3 Hands are together and fingers are spread to maximise chances of making an effective smother.

4 Head is kept directly behind the hands and forearms for protection.

5 Eyes are fixed firmly on the ball to ensure the smother covers the ball and to improve chances of gaining possession after the ball has been smothered.

INSPIRATIONAL: Former North Melbourne captain Adam Simpson demonstrates a classic smother.

Spoil

//// Graham Johncock likes to take a mark, but knows how and when to spoil when the situation arises. He also aims to turn defence into attack by directing the ball to a teammate.

When Adelaide's Graham Johncock attempts to spoil his opponent in a marking contest, he always follows the team rule – make sure the ball goes forward.

The Crows work hard to get numbers back in defence when the opposition is in possession and Johncock tries to direct his spoil towards his teammates on the ground.

"You try to have a bit of control over the spoil," he said. "You don't want it to go off the fist and fall anywhere. You try to make sure you know where your ground-cover players are and hit the ball in their vicinity."

Since 2007, defenders have had to be careful not to infringe against the forward, with the strict interpretation of the hands-in-the-back rule.

"They've been touchy on that rule," Johncock said. "Everyone knows if you put your hand in the back of the opposition, you'll have a free kick paid against you. I think a lot of players are still getting used to it, with three or four of those situations being paid at every game each week."

Since making his debut with the Crows in 2002, Johncock has been used at both ends of the ground.

As a forward, he has the same mindset as he does as a defender when he is behind his opponent. "If I'm getting outmuscled by my opponent and he's in a better position than me to mark the ball, I'd better make sure that it comes to ground," he said.

But if he is in the clear, the Crow is happy to go for the mark rather than spoil.

EYES ON THE BALL

Spoiling is an effective method of preventing an opponent from marking or gaining possession of the ball. When attempting to spoil the football away in a marking contest, it is imperative the player maintains eye contact on the football at all times. If he takes his eyes off the ball in a marking contest and makes contact with the player attempting to mark, a free kick will be awarded.

"If the ball is there and you're in the right position to take the mark, then (you) back yourself in to take the mark," he said. "But a lot of forwards like to play in front of defenders and, if you're a defender, you try to bring the ball to ground."

The Crows do a lot of one-on-one work at training when they can practise their spoiling technique. "I get some confidence out of that and try to take it into games. It definitely helps," Johncock said.

When he started in the AFL, one player he respected as a defender was former Port Adelaide captain and Brownlow medallist Gavin Wanganeen.

"He was a pretty courageous backman who took big marks and took on the best forwards in the competition," he said.

Two of the better exponents of the spoil in the modern era have been former full-backs Stephen Silvagni (Carlton) and Mick Martyn (North Melbourne and Carlton), thwarting many attacks with a timely fist. Veteran Essendon defender Dustin Fletcher has also pulled off some athletic spoils in his career.

AT MAXIMUM REACH

Graham Johncock has his eyes firmly focused on the ball and at no stage has placed his hands in the back of West Coast's **David Wirrpanda**. As the ball has arrived, Johncock has fully extended his arm for maximum reach and, using a clenched fist, has punched the ball away from the hands of his opponent. It is important that Johncock does not fall into the back of his opponent and keeps his feet to follow up the ball after spoiling it away. Ideally, if in the defensive section of the ground, Johncock should be aiming to spoil the ball towards the boundary line.

PROVIDING A CLEAR PASSAGE

Jarrad Waite is an excellent shepherder and blocker, regularly creating opportunities for his teammates to break free with the ball. Here he puts himself between teammate **Nick Stevens** and Richmond's **Jordan McMahon** as Stevens breaks clear with the ball. Waite makes solid body contact, pushing strongly off his left leg and using his right arm firmly against the opponent to increase the blocking area and to ensure McMahon cannot get around him. He lets his teammate know what is around him.

Shepherd

//// **Carlton's Jarrad Waite is a leader in the art of shepherding and blocking. He explains the importance of clearing the path for a teammate.**

The one-percenters such as shepherding/blocking have been an important part of Carlton star Jarrad Waite's game since he was a young player growing up in country Victoria.

Waite is one of the leading exponents of the shepherd/block in the AFL and sees it as an important skill in the modern game.

"It's pretty useful in that it just helps your team out, but I don't check how many blocks I've had each week," the Blue said.

"I believe it's pretty important and if someone does a good block, we'll bring it up in our review."

A good shepherd/block is the difference between a perfect pass from skipper Chris Judd or vice-captain Nick Stevens to leading full-forward Brendan Fevola, or an errant kick that is too high and allows the defence to make a spoil.

"You do want the ball in the hands of the good users of the footy and our midfielders are generally the good users at the club," Waite said.

His primary objective is to provide a clear pathway for a teammate. "You try to make sure you get in between your immediate opponent and the player you're trying to protect," he said.

"You try to take the opponent out of the contest, so your player can run and get away a little bit easier than if he's got a man right behind him."

When making the shepherd/block, Waite tries to ensure he does not make illegal contact with his opponent, particularly around the head. "The AFL has shown that part of the body is sacrosanct," he said.

"You have to make sure you make good body contact when you take the player out. It is good for the team if you see one of your teammates make a good block."

The Blues practise this skill at most sessions, often when they are doing a handball drill.

"While it's not mainstream, it's one of those skills that is vital to your team going well," he said. "You don't want to take your teammates out in training, but it gives you that practice and hopefully in a game you make the block each time."

Waite said it was important to communicate with teammates to ensure that the shepherd/block was applied effectively.

TEAM MAN: Waite provides protection for teammate Heath Scotland against Fremantle.

TEACHING POINTS

Shepherding/blocking is one of the game's major team skills. A player can be legally shepherded as long as the ball is not more than five metres away. A shepherd is performed by using the body and arms to protect a teammate.

1. Get between your teammate and the opponent, but not too close.

2. Assume a brace position.

3. Fingers are outstretched and arms spread below the shoulder – do not hold your opponent.

4. Talk to your teammate to tell him he is clear.

Bump

//// Players have to make a split-second decision about whether to tackle or bump, but executing the perfect bump can have a positive effect on the team. But it must be within the rules and the player's head has to be protected at all times.

As a run-with player, the bump is an important part of Fremantle hard man Ryan Crowley's game.

Crowley relishes the in-close, physical stuff and works hard on those aspects of the game.

"A lot of my training focuses on when I don't have the ball," the Docker said. "We have a tackling coach and I work with him a fair bit. Bumping and tackling are a big part of my game because a lot of the time

I'm not expected to have the ball. I'm trying to stop someone from getting the ball."

Crowley said bumping came naturally to him as a player who enjoys physical contact. "A lot of guys will go through a whole season without laying a bump because it doesn't come naturally to them," he said.

In days gone by, bumping was an instinctive skill employed by players to either dispossess their opponent or clear

1 **PREPARATION**
Bumping often occurs as players approach or look to gain possession of the football. It is important players who are gaining possession of the football always keep their eyes on the ball.

2 **BRACE**
Crowley has gained possession of the ball and is now bracing himself for a bump. He continues to stay low, has feet apart, knees bent and has his body weight moving forward.

3 **IMPACT**
At the impact point, he tenses his muscles to form a strong rigid surface. He will tuck his elbow in close to his body and will lead with his shoulder.

4 **RECOVERY**
Once the bump has been completed, Crowley will continue to move forward and work to maintain his balance.

a path for a teammate. With umpires instructed to protect the player's head at all times, Crowley admits he has to think carefully and assess the situation before employing the bump.

"In the past you would just do it instinctively, whereas now there is that split second when you think, 'Am I going to get into trouble for this?'" Crowley said. "In the past when you might have tried to bump someone, now you might prop and corral them, with a view to laying a tackle.

"One that has almost gone out completely is when you're going to get to the ball second and you're coming straight on to the player who is going to pick the

ball up. In the past you might have been able to get to their shoulder."

Crowley said the best way to lay a bump in the modern game was from side-on.

"Front-on and from behind is impossible," he said. "The majority of bumps happen these days when two players commit to bump each other. Very rarely do you see one guy run straight through another guy when he's not ready for it."

Crowley believes Hawthorn vice-captain Luke Hodge is the best exponent of the bump he has played against, although he admits it was not pleasant being on the wrong side of a couple delivered by the recently retired Byron Pickett.

"Luke Hodge has amazing strength and Byron Pickett was pretty brutal when he got them right," Crowley said. "When he gets it right, Dean Solomon at our club is as good at the bump as I've seen."

As an avid Collingwood fan growing up in Victoria, Crowley's idol was former Magpie captain Gavin Brown, who also enjoyed the physical side of the game.

"He was pretty hard at it and never took a backward step," he said.

Crowley has also watched other AFL players such as Essendon's Mark McVeigh, and Sydney's Brett Kirk deliver the perfect bump while retired Brisbane Lions Chris and Brad Scott were tough as nails when it came to bumping.

HARD EDGE: Alastair Clarkson's belief in a relentless, disciplined approach within his team has paid rich dividends, guiding Hawthorn to a premiership in 2008.

07
Coaching skills

//// **Coaches come in all forms – motivators, strategists, teachers, disciplinarians. The best in the business manage to combine all of those traits in games and at training.**

It is hard to imagine Australian Football without a coach but the earliest forms of the game were without any type of formal direction from the sidelines.

Usually, the captain guided the team and records show that Collingwood was the first VFL club to name a coach when it appointed Billy Strickland coach in 1904. Previously he had been captain and, like most captains of the time, the role was more about organisation than structure. Certainly there was no suggestion of tactics or game-plans.

While Strickland was the first 'official' coach to be named, it is generally acknowledged that the first League coach was Carlton's Jack Worrall.

Worrall was a man ahead of his time and his record at Carlton, and later Essendon, is worthy of note. He coached Carlton to three premierships (1906-08) and Essendon to two (1911-12) and even coached the VFL umpires at one stage.

Given Worrall's success, it was no surprise that the role of the coach started to grow in the early 1900s. These

included Arch Hosie, who was appointed Port Adelaide's first coach in the SANFL in 1908. Like Strickland, Hosie had been captain and most reports of the late 1800s indicated that the captain was the person in charge of a side.

Australian Football Hall of Fame member Jack 'Dinny' Reedman was appointed West Adelaide's coach in 1908, leading the club to a premiership and the Championship of Australia in that season.

Jack Williams (Subiaco in 1905-07) was the earliest known coach in Western Australia, followed by William Plunkett (East Perth, 1906) and James Kennedy (East Perth, 1907-08).

As the role of the coach expanded, so too did the talent and knowledge base.

In Victoria, legendary Collingwood coach Jock McHale built a record over four decades and 714 games that will probably never be beaten. Other coaching luminaries, including Norm Smith, Frank 'Checker' Hughes, John Kennedy, Allan Jeans, Ron Barassi, Tom Hafey, David Parkin, Kevin Sheedy, Leigh Matthews and Mick Malthouse,

followed him. South Australia has also produced some of the finest coaches the game has seen: Jack Oatey, Fos Williams, John Cahill and through to the modern day via Port Adelaide coach Mark Williams and his Adelaide counterpart Neil Craig.

Phillip Matson was widely regarded as a coach ahead of his time in Western Australia in the early 1900s and his record allowed him to be inducted to the Australian Hall of Fame in 2004. Other outstanding WA coaches included Haydn Bunton jnr, Johnny Leonard, Jack Sheedy and John Todd.

Today, the coach is surrounded by a team of assistants and has the latest in tactics, planning, technology, psychology and sports science at his disposal. That makes Western Bulldogs coach Rodney Eade an ideal person to discuss the modern-day senior coach.

Brendan McCartney, a long-time assistant coach at Geelong and Richmond, sets up many of the Cats' skills sessions and he looks at that aspect of coaching.

Senior coach

//// While the buck normally stops with the senior coach, his role has expanded over the years as the game has become more professional and technologically advanced.

It's hard to believe it was not until the early 1990s that most AFL senior coaches were employed by their clubs on a full-time basis.

Nowadays, your typical senior coach heads up a team that includes at least four full-time assistant coaches, along with additional development, skills and fitness coaches. In searching for an edge over his side's coming opponent, he also works extraordinarily long weeks that would put most corporate professionals to shame.

Western Bulldogs senior coach Rodney Eade, a four-time Hawthorn premiership player under coaching luminaries John Kennedy, David Parkin and Allan Jeans, said senior coaches today not only had to be master tacticians, they also had to be master managers and delegators.

"With the amount of footy staff at clubs today, it's very important that you're a good manager – it's mainly about communication and making sure you're getting around and chatting to everyone," Eade said.

"You've also got to delegate a lot and have a lot of confidence and trust in your staff members – you just can't do it all yourself."

A strong work ethic is essential too.

Eade, who was Sydney senior coach from 1996-2002 (152 games, 81 wins, 69 losses, 2 draws, winning percentage 53 per cent) before joining the Western Bulldogs ahead of the 2005 season, said his preparation for a match starts almost immediately after the siren has sounded on the previous week's game.

"It's a pretty full-on week, not only at the club, you're obviously doing a fair bit at home, preparing for the game ahead and watching other teams play," he said.

Aside from an immediate post-match review with his match committee, Eade's week consists of: further reviews of the game with the match committee and his players; numerous meetings dissecting his side's coming opponents and instructing his players on the tactics, match-ups and their specific roles for that game; and overseeing two main training sessions that are generally designed to reinforce the set plays and game style planned for that weekend.

Fortunately, Eade says it is easy for coaches to keep abreast of any new tactics being introduced by opposition clubs.

"You're watching that much football and you look at games from a coaching perspective where you're looking for different things – positional plays, game styles etc – so you generally pick most things up," he said.

Eade said, as professional as players had become, a senior coach still had a motivational role to play.

"Players are very professional so you give them a lot of feedback, information and education during the week, but we're all human and we all like a cause and being part of a team," he said.

"So they can respond to something like a motivational story. You can't make the football club too sterile and clinical, players still need different stimuli."

MAKING A POINT:
Senior coach Rodney
Eade delivers his
message to the
Western Bulldogs.

THE TEACHER:
Like many assistant
coaches, Geelong's
Brendan McCartney paints
his players a clear picture
of what is required.

Skills coach

//// Skills coaches have a vital role to play in today's AFL. Entrusted with their club's brightest young prospects, they need to be part analyst, part teacher and part mentor.

No matter how decorated a player's junior career and no matter how well-rounded his game may appear, once drafted he will go to his new club with skill deficiencies that will have to be overcome if he wants to make it in the AFL.

That's where the clubs' skills and development coaches such as Geelong's Brendan McCartney have a vital role to play.

McCartney, a long-time assistant coach at Geelong and before that at Richmond, has worked extensively with young players on their skills. He said clubs were almost always aware of a player's deficiencies before drafting him, so the real skill was not in identifying those deficiencies but in creating a program that focuses on the skills they needed to develop to overcome them.

"Even the very best youngsters invariably need some modification to their games," McCartney said.

"The way you deliver that – what you say, how you say it – is important, but the content is the crucial thing.

"Before you can do anything, your coaching program has got to have a clear picture of the skills that a player needs to develop to be able to play in their position, be that as a tall defender, inside midfielder or small forward."

Only then does a skills coach's teaching ability come into play and it is primarily young players' kicking, transition skills and body positioning that require remedial work, according to McCartney.

"We teach them all the different types of kicks – when to kick it hard and flat and when to keep a little bit off the kick – which are so crucial for you to be able to beat the opposition's defence," he said.

"Then there's the transition skills, being able to adjust from different parts of the game, from attack to defence and from defence to attack.

"And the other main one is body positioning skills, teaching players the proper way to attack the ball in a contest, so they do it safely and build physical and mental confidence."

Obviously, each player learns at a different rate, so a coach needs to be able to quickly build an understanding of how each individual learns.

"You've got to tap into how they learn, create the environment they need to learn in," McCartney said.

"That's the challenge for any good coaching program, to create the environment and feedback mechanisms where a player can see where he's at, so he can sense any improvement, or areas where he's still got a way to go."

Which begs the question: how then does a skills coach learn such skills?

McCartney said nothing could replace on-the-job experience.

"There's no secret or trick to coaching. The longer you're in it, the more actual hours of face-to-face coaching and game analysis you put in, the more you develop your skills and your knowledge," he said.

"Being around coaches that are good teachers, like 'Bomber' (Mark Thompson) who works closely with his coaches at Geelong to develop them as teachers, is also really important."

QUICK LEARNER: With the assistance of the development coaches at Collingwood, Irishman Marty Clarke has made a lightning transition to Australian Football to follow in the footsteps of fellow countrymen Jim Stynes and Tadhg Kennelly.

08
Preparation

//// **Plenty of work goes on behind the scenes before the players run out on the field each weekend. The hard grind begins on the training track.**

The football vernacular is full of buzz words and phrases – particularly in modern times – but one that stands the test of time is 'preparation'.

It might have changed slightly from the 1960s when then Carlton star Ron Barassi, wearing the whitest of white shorts on his Saturday morning football segment, advised young players to polish their boots and tie their laces correctly. If you can't be a footballer, at least look like one.

Today, those sentiments about preparing remain the same. Do the hard work and careful planning beforehand and the results will follow.

For some, however, it means preparing for a totally different code.

But it's not as simple as deciding overnight to give up one sport and take on a game as physically demanding as Australian Football. Often players are making huge sacrifices, both personally and physically, to abandon one career path and turn their attention to our game.

In recent times, Australian Football has attracted highly skilled and athletic players from Ireland where Gaelic Football enjoys a similar standing and has links to Australian Football.

Former Melbourne champion Jim Stynes has been the biggest success story in the so-called 'Irish experiment', playing a major role in the rise of the Demons through the late 1980s and into the 1990s.

More recently, former Swan Tadhg Kennelly delighted fans with his run and dash. Kennelly was given a football to take everywhere with him when he first arrived and spent countless hours perfecting his kicking technique.

Australian Football also competes with other sports to attract the best players and athletes it can and sometimes those players require just as much skill development as a player from overseas starting from scratch.

Port Adelaide premiership ruckman Dean Brogan played in the National Basketball League before deciding to reignite his love of Australian Football.

While he had the advantage of being tall, Brogan still had to work on his skills, having played football only at junior level before abandoning his basketball career in the late 1990s.

Learning new skills is one thing – practising them is another. Adelaide's Tyson Edwards is a perfect example of a player who has fought his way to the top by continually working on his skills and practising them.

You can always learn by simply watching the game and that's something former Collingwood champion Nathan Buckley did throughout his career and continues now in his role as a commentator.

And it's not just about developing skills or switching codes: coming back from injury – as Essendon's champion full-forward Matthew Lloyd will attest – takes a great deal of preparation.

Then there is preparation of another kind - getting ready to umpire a game. Leading AFL umpire Scott McLaren has some good advice for aspiring umpires about officiating our game.

FAST LEARNER:
Tadhg Kennelly worked
tirelessly with the skills
coaches at the Swans to
become one of the best
defenders in the AFL.

Starting from scratch

//// Tadhg Kennelly was such a key part of the Sydney side between 2001-08 that it is hard to believe it took him just under two years to acquire the skills necessary to reach the elite level.

Tadhg Kennelly has a simple piece of advice for any young Irishmen thinking about moving half-way across the world to try their luck in the AFL: your heart has to be in it.

He's emphasising that if you want to learn to play Australian Football from scratch, above all you have to have the burning desire to do it.

"I just wanted to do it, wanted to do it, wanted to do it," Kennelly stressed.

"I basically lived AFL football for a couple of years. I had a footy in my hands all the time, I did skills three times a day, every day. I was just driven to do it."

Kennelly joined the Swans as an 18-year-old rookie late in 1999 after being spotted at an under-17 International Rules carnival. While he had already mapped out an amateur career playing Gaelic Football in Ireland, the AFL offered him the chance to be a full-time sportsman, which was too tempting to ignore.

The things Kennelly found hardest to grasp in his crash course on football were handling the oval ball and tackling – a round ball is used in Gaelic Football and tackling is outlawed. Developing the strength, bulk and endurance to play AFL also required plenty of hard work.

While Kennelly said the tactics in both games were "very, very similar", he had difficulty picking up some of football's jargon. "In my first few years when 'Rocket' (Rodney Eade) was coach, he said to me one day, 'Hell, Tadhg, bomb it long down the guts' and I'm thinking, 'What on earth is he talking about?'"

TRIUMPHANT: Kennelly celebrates the Swans' breakthrough premiership win in 2005.

But as with most aspects of Australian Football, Kennelly was a fast learner. So much so that after two years of tireless one-on-one skills work with the Swans' assistant coaches – particularly George Stone, who Kennelly said "basically taught (him) the game" – playing football started to feel "natural rather than mechanical". "Suddenly the penny just drops and you just grab the footy and kick it without thinking about it," he said. "That's when you just think, 'The sky's the limit here'."

However, Kennelly said there was one advantage about coming to the AFL from a non-football background. Not knowing the game's history, and more particularly the standing of your senior teammates in the competition, made your transition easier.

"When I started, I was training with Paul Kelly, Andrew Dunkley, Tony Lockett and Daryn Cresswell – all big names in the game – but coming from Ireland I didn't know them and I wasn't in awe," he said.

"As a normal 18-year-old Australian coming into the football club there would be a sense of intimidation when you trained with these blokes.

"But I just started busting my gut against them in training, which helped my development a lot."

While Kennelly has returned to Ireland and fulfil his ambition to play Gaelic Football at the highest level in his homeland, he left an indelible mark on our game and has provided an inspiration for others to follow in his footsteps.

HOW TADHG MADE IT

With a fierce determination to succeed in the AFL, Tadhg Kennelly quickly mastered Australian Football via:

1. Intensive one-on-one skills sessions with Swans assistant coaches.
2. Specialised tackling drills.
3. Weight training sessions to build strength.
4. Extra distance running to improve his endurance.
5. Team meetings on strategies and game-plans.

PERFECT FIT:
Dean Brogan's mobility, hand-eye coordination and ball skills have enabled him to make the switch from basketball to the AFL. Here he battles with Swans ruckman Darren Jolly.

Switching sports

//// **With many sporting options now available to youngsters, and the AFL recruiting net being cast far and wide, more athletes are switching to Australian Football.**

When Port Adelaide ruckman Dean Brogan took the victory dais to receive his AFL premiership medallion in 2004, he completed a unique double in Australian sport. Already the owner of a National Basketball League championship ring with the Adelaide 36ers in 1998, the big man had reached the summit of two vastly different sports in a remarkably short timeframe.

Brogan's decision to swap from basketball to football was somewhat forced, owing to the bankruptcy of his new team the Newcastle Falcons in 1999. Back home in Adelaide, the youngster pulled on the boots for South Adelaide in the SANFL initially as a simple distraction.

Importantly, Brogan was already familiar with the oval ball, having played with South Adelaide's under-17 side and regularly kicked around with mates in downtime at the Australian Institute of Sport.

"Obviously, the basics of kicking, hitting targets and reading the play took time to master, but the more you play, the better you get," Brogan said. "I also got along to a lot of AFL games and watched tapes of the really good ruckmen around the league."

The most difficult part of his transition proved to be the gruelling physical nature of Australian Football.

"Basketball is pretty much a non-contact sport, and going from the small dimensions of a basketball court to a football oval created a lot more wear and tear on the body," he said.

FAST BREAK: Brogan won an NBL championship ring with the Adelaide 36ers.

Despite this, Brogan's mobility, hand-eye coordination and ball skills attracted the attention of AFL talent scouts, earning him a place on Port Adelaide's rookie list in 2000. But his football conditioning had only just begun.

"For the first year or two at Port, I really struggled backing up from games – it would take me four or five days to get over it. I wasn't used to all of the bumps and bruises you pick up," he said.

Brogan's advice for those attempting a switch is to get your body 'football fit'.

"Most people who go from basketball to football have a lot of groin problems, and if I had my time over again, I'd do more

injury-prevention work, because you're going to do a lot of running and get hit more, so you've got to be strong through your hips and stomach area.

"Gone are the days of trying to have the biggest biceps. Now it's more core stability and injury prevention; things like pilates, yoga and functional weights."

Good listening skills are also essential to fit as seamlessly as possible into the macho, heavily team-orientated football environment.

"Basketball is very individualised and Americanised, so it was a big shock to come over to a football culture that is so mentally and physically tough. In my first couple of years, I whinged and complained a lot and really struggled with it," Brogan said. "Luckily, I had great ruckmen like Matthew Primus, Brendon Lade and Barnaby French teaching me, and Port were really patient with my development.

"The best thing to do is keep your ear to the ground, keep your mouth shut and just learn as much as you can."

MAKING THE TRANSITION

1 Immerse yourself in the game with relentless practice and training, as well as watching live games and video footage of the best players in action.

2 Get your body 'football fit' with exercises focusing on core stability and injury prevention.

3 Become team-orientated in everything you do, enacting the instructions of coaches without complaint.

Practising the skills

//// Adelaide's Tyson Edwards has become one of the AFL's premier midfielders by honing and refining every area of his game with relentless work on the training track.

Tyson Edwards has developed into one of the most efficient users of the football, earning him the respect and plaudits of his peers and coaches. Like most good judges, he believes the bulk of skill work must be done early on.

"The younger the better for kids to learn," Edwards said, citing former Hawthorn and Adelaide star Darren Jarman as a prime example of practice makes perfect. "Darren stands out as the most skilful guy I've seen, and he was able to get to that level from hours and hours of just kicking the footy when he was younger."

Jarman was fortunate to have talented older brother Andrew to kick around with at a young age, and Edwards highly recommends such companions for budding footballers. But as this is not always feasible, there are many ways to improvise.

"Pick out simple targets in the backyard or at the local park, and just try to hit them over and over again," said Edwards, who began his AFL career in 1995.

"That's what I did as a youngster when I didn't have anyone else to kick with. Try different sorts of kicks, change up the targets and make it fun as well – see how many times you can hit something in a row, for example."

Self-improvement, however, is not limited to juniors. Recently, Edwards identified and rectified a weakness in his game.

"A couple of years ago, I noticed I wasn't kicking goals from outside 45 metres,"

the dual premiership player said. "It was something I wasn't really confident with, because I'm not an overly long kick. So I started putting in the time and asking the coaches a few questions, and one thing I worked out I was doing was simply trying to kick the ball too hard, and that I was leaning over the kick too much.

"So I started to relax, lean back on the kick a bit more and concentrated on actually pointing my toe with the kick – you seem to get more distance that way. Eventually, I was able to feel more comfortable and get some better results by working on those things."

Aside from mastery of the skill itself, relentless practice with specific areas also gives footballers the confidence to execute the skill when it matters most – under pressure in a big-game situation.

Edwards strongly believes skill development should also take place off the training track.

"You can watch endless video footage of great players, and I've done a bit of that; guys who dominate at stoppages and how they position themselves, or the ones who are really good at tackling," he said.

It may be a cliché, but Edwards cannot stress enough the importance of being able to kick equally well with either foot.

"I see a lot of the younger kids coming into the AFL now who are predominantly one-sided," he said. "If you're two-sided, it gives you a bit more time, and the way the game has quickened up in the last three or four years, you don't have a lot of time out on the ground. It just gives you a lot more options."

GETTING BETTER: Edwards fine-tunes his hand skills at training.

FOOTY FOOTAGE

Edwards believes the correct technique must be mastered before you can set about practising your skills, and he even reinforces this with young sons Jackson, Luke and Brodie.

"Most people these days have a video camera, so sometimes when I'm having a kick with the boys in the backyard, I'll videotape them," Edwards said. "I know when I was growing up that I didn't always listen to what my parents were saying, but if you can actually see what you're doing wrong, you can understand it so much better."

BALANCED APPROACH:
Tyson Edwards has worked
hard on being proficient on
both sides of his body.

Learning by watching

//// Nathan Buckley prided himself on learning by watching, courtesy of his considerable powers of observation and a rare ability to identify and rectify weaknesses in his game.

People prefer to learn in different ways. Some prefer to read, some prefer to listen and some prefer whiteboard explanations, while some such as Collingwood great Nathan Buckley prefer to watch a physical demonstration.

"But the method isn't as important as your attitude to it," Buckley said. "You need to be open to the opportunity of learning, accept the fact you can *always* improve, that the product you are at any given time is not the best you can be, and be prepared to test your limits."

Buckley loved watching and analysing teammates and opponents to glean information that might help him and his club.

When he arrived at Collingwood at the end of 1993, he identified Tony Shaw as the club's hardest trainer and tried to duplicate everything Shaw did on the track. Buckley also used another teammate, Gavin Brown, as a role model for how to attack the ball. He admits: "It was an area of the game that didn't come naturally to me and while very few players ever achieve Browny's level of ferocity, the fact I aspired to it was an improvement in itself."

Buckley also improved the efficiency of his disposals around stoppages by paying close attention to St Kilda star Robert Harvey. Early in his career, Buckley would wheel out of a pack and generally bomb it to the longest contested situation. Watching the Saints was pivotal to his education. He noticed Nathan Burke doing the same thing he was and contrasted it with the approach of Harvey, who backed himself to evade

an opponent, create some run and maybe hit a leading target. "From the moment I made that realisation, I tried to emulate that aspect of Harvey's game, along with his non-stop running," he said.

Others he admired included his two other great peers, former Brisbane Lions skipper Michael Voss for his physical approach and competitiveness, and former Essendon captain James Hird for his desperation and decision making. He was also impressed with their leadership qualities.

Buckley said the best way to learn is to go to a match because television merely shows the action directly around the ball and you can't fully appreciate important aspects such as work-rate, decision making and skill execution. "For example, it might appear Lance Franklin has received an easy ball on a lead when it was actually his third lead and the result of a lot of hard work," he said.

He suggests going to games with mates with a specific purpose. "You might decide: 'Let's watch (Carlton skipper) Chris Judd to see how he deals with his tagger and where he runs on the field,' and during the game you might discuss your observations, and you're learning the whole time," he said.

Then it's a case of how to use the information and apply it to your own game. "Don't be afraid to try something and fail at first," Buckley said. "Always challenge yourself."

The possibilities are endless. "The data is all around you, from coaches, teammates, opponents, etc.," he said. "So keep your ears and eyes open for the next opportunity to learn and improve."

MENTOR: Buckley passes on his knowledge as an assistant coach for Australia's International Rules team during the two-Test series against Ireland in 2008.

ASTUTE OBSERVER: Buckley, pictured with fellow commentator Bruce McAvaney, has earned widespread praise for his role on Channel Seven.

OPPOSITE PAGE: Nathan Buckley owes his status as arguably Collingwood's greatest player to his endless quest for perfection, watching and analysing teammates and opponents.

BACK TO HIS BEST:
Essendon spearhead
Matthew Lloyd takes the
Toyota AFL Mark of the Year
in round 18, 2008, against
Melbourne at the MCG.

Coming back from injury

//// The longer you play sport, the greater your chances of injury. The recovery and rehabilitation process is crucial to returning to the field effectively.

Round three, 2006: Essendon's Matthew Lloyd rips his hamstring off the bone against the Western Bulldogs. The captain's season is finished before it really began, and a long and arduous recovery begins.

Lloyd returns fit and fired-up for the 2007 season opener, going on to boot 62 goals for the year, and following up with several career-defining performances in 2008.

Here, the Bomber champion outlines the key strategies to a successful comeback:

"Initially, you'll feel helpless. But you can't just walk around with your tail between your legs, because there are a lot of people who can draw off you negatively. You've just got to get on with the business of rehabbing.

"Motivation can be tough. But, just like you'd do in a normal football season, you need to set goals in the first few weeks of your injury – maybe firstly to start jogging, then running, kicking and so on. It keeps you going and makes you appreciate the game much more as well.

"Don't rush things. You've got to give respect to your injury, whether it's a four-week or a one-year hamstring. I've had hamstrings where at times I've thought, 'I'm sore, but I'll see if I can get through it'. But now I know my body's telling me something.

"Seek out people with similar experiences. You might learn how they kept themselves going. Also, stay involved in the club as much as you can, even though you're not playing; get along to team meetings, into the dressing room, game days, training – just stay with it.

"Avoid bad eating habits. You've got to be preparing yourself like you're still playing

LOW POINT: Lloyd is assisted from the field after suffering a serious hamstring injury in 2006.

AFL, as it's just going to be harder later on if you let yourself go. If you're out for an extended period, it's the little things that you do when no one is looking that really matter.

"You'll regain your confidence on the training track. Once you've been given the green light, throw yourself into everything at training – twisting, turning, flying for your marks; all of the things you would do in a match. Then it takes only one or two involvements in an actual game and you'll forget you were even injured."

LLOYD'S BEST ADVICE

"With injuries, so many different people can tell you so many different things, whether it be your parents, an uncle, or a mate outside the club. Someone I saw at a local club was rubbing Deep Heat into a hamstring injury, which is the worst thing you can do. The key is to only listen to the people who have the knowledge."

TAKING CONTROL:
Scott McLaren says
umpires need to get
their message across in
a clear, concise manner.

Umpiring

//// From youngsters overseeing local leagues to the men at AFL level, umpires require a unique set of skills to be effective in a pressurised, unforgiving environment.

Scott McLaren is better placed than most to impart knowledge on the art of umpiring. After taking it up as a means of earning extra "pocket money" as a teenager, McLaren has officiated in more than 300 AFL games, including five Grand Finals, a State-of-Origin match and an International Rules Series fixture.

According to McLaren, who made his debut at senior AFL level in 1994, the first requirement for any umpire in today's fast-paced game is supreme fitness. "We've worn GPS devices a few times and worked out that we run about 15 kilometres on average in a game," he said. However, running ability alone does not translate into performance, with the ability to know where to run equally important.

"You've got to have a 'footy feel' as well, a pretty strong understanding of the game," McLaren said. "You need to know where the ball is going and get to the right position. It's quite often hard for players who take up umpiring, because they're used to exclusively watching the ball, whereas umpires watch the players."

Heavy criticism from players on the field, fans and the media is an inevitable aspect of the role, meaning a thick skin and a positive outlook are essential.

"Umpiring can be a very negative environment; people only look for the things you do wrong and don't care about the 25 good free kicks you paid for the day. They'll want to focus on the 50/50 one that might have been wrong," he said.

"Even though others might not rate you highly, you have to believe in yourself and

READY FOR ACTION: McLaren leads the umpires on to the field to start the game.

your ability. We don't listen too much to what outside people say, we just umpire for our coaches and our colleagues, and only take on board the feedback we get from them."

On that point, McLaren stresses the need for umpires to listen closely to their official observers and not become defensive when constructive criticism

is being offered. Verbal communication skills can also make life much easier for a whistle-blower, especially when a situation is threatening to erupt on the field.

"You have to get your message across quickly, clearly and concisely, because there's no time to mess around out there," McLaren said. "You need someone to be in control, because the players can be ranting and raving and questioning every decision under the sun, and if you get into a slanging match, it's not going to do anyone any good. We must be calm, composed and measured at all times."

As with players, at the end of the day it is consistency that AFL umpires aim for, striving to achieve decision accuracy and bouncing percentages above 90 per cent.

"You're just trying to turn in week-in, week-out performances that are very solid – whether you've got injury niggles, a cold or whatever," he said. "You can't afford to have an off week, because every single decision is under so much scrutiny."

HONEST ASSESSMENT

Self-appraisal through video footage of matches can be a key to improvement as an umpire. After each round, AFL umpires are given DVDs of their performance, which have been dubbed with their on-field communication with players. By the time their Monday night coaching review comes around, most umpires will already know which of their decisions were correct, how well they positioned themselves at contests, and whether they communicated effectively.

AFL coaching managers

AUSTRALIAN FOOTBALL LEAGUE
Manager Coaching, Umpiring & Volunteers
AFL Development
GPO BOX 1449
Melbourne VIC 3001
afl.com.au
Lawrie.Woodman@afl.com.au
(03) 9643 1999

NSW/ACT
State Coaching Manager
AFL (NSW/ACT)
PO BOX 333
Strawberry Hills NSW 2012
aflnswact.com.au
Daniel.Archer@aflnswact.com.au
(02) 8333 8020

SOUTH AUSTRALIA
Coaching Manager
SANFL
PO BOX 1
West Lakes SA 5021
sanfl.com.au
roberto@sanfl.com.au
(08) 8424 2286

VICTORIA
Coaching Development Manager
AFL Victoria
GPO BOX 4337
Melbourne VIC 3001
aflvic.com.au
steve.teakel@aflvic.com.au
(03) 8663 3015

NORTHERN TERRITORY
Game Development/Talent Manager
AFLNT
PO BOX AFLNT 1
Casuarina NT 0811
aflnt.com.au
jchipperfield@aflnt.com.au
(08) 8945 2224

QUEENSLAND
State Training Manager
AFL Queensland
PO BOX 1211
Coorparoo DC QLD 4151
aflq.com.au
deanm@aflq.com.au
(07) 3394 2433

TASMANIA
State Manager Coach Education
AFL Tasmania
PO Box 1896
Launceston TAS 7250
footballtas.com.au
nprobert@footballtas.com.au
(03) 6230 1806

WESTERN AUSTRALIA
Talent & Coaching Coordinator
WAFC
PO BOX 275
Subiaco WA 6904
wafootball.com.au
rguadagnino@wafc.com.au
(08) 9381 5599